Meditation
&Life

THE *Self-Discovery* SERIES

Meditation &Life

By
SWAMI CHINMAYANANDA

CHINMAYA PUBLICATIONS WEST

Chinmaya Publications
Main Office
P.O. Box 129
Piercy, CA 95587, USA

Chinmaya Publications
Distribution Office
560 Bridgetown Pike
Langhorne, PA 19053, USA

Central Chinmaya Mission Trust
Sandeepany Sadhanalaya
Saki Vihar Road
Bombay, India 400 072

Second Printing 1995

Earlier editions of the present work have been published by Central Chinmaya Mission Trust. Chapters 27 through 38 of the present work have appeared earlier as the book *Hasten Slowly*, published in 1972 in India by Central Chinmaya Mission Trust.

Credits:

Cover design by Peter Tucker
Photo of Swami Chinmayananda on the back cover
   by Joy Von Tiedemann
Photo page ii by Anjli Singh

Library of Congress Catalog Card Number 91-77690

ISBN 1-880687-00-3

Contents

Part Two
THE PROCESS OF MEDITATION

Part Three
AIDS TO MEDITATION

Part Four
HASTEN SLOWLY

mutually destructive

Preface

"Our physical, mental, intellectual, and spiritual personalities must be blended into one harmonious whole. Meditation is the technique for achieving this harmony. It is the highest spiritual discipline. Through meditation we come to experience peace within ourselves. Internecine wars between desires end. Conflicts between duties no longer torment us. The mind is able to view life as a whole."

Swami Chinmayananda

Many of us are overwhelmed by the complexity of our lives today. Because of that complexity, many seek to escape the pain and the pressure through a variety of means—through work or play or a combination of both. The tradition of spiritual thought called Vedanta advises us not to escape from life, but teaches us instead how to maintain a high quality of life through intelligent understanding of the true nature of existence.

In *Meditation and Life*, Swami Chinmayananda, one of the greatest teachers of Vedanta in modern times, takes us step by step through the thought process required to reestablish mastery over our lives, beginning with the world within. The instrument we use in our life experiences, says the author, is not the body, as we generally assume, but the mind. The state of our lives depends on the state of our mind. We all are familiar with the anguish we feel when our minds race uncontrollably around some worry, some experienced hurt, or some anticipated fear. Our minds manage to create a hell around us. As we learn to tame our minds into fit instruments of experience, step by step we gain control over our lives. No matter what our outer circumstances may be, with our minds controlled, we are the masters of the situation: we can *choose* to live in joy.

This is what meditation teaches us. *Meditation and Life* takes us through the logic behind meditation, as well as the specific techniques of applying meditative practice to our daily lives. Swami Chinmayananda shows us how, by gaining mastery over our inner lives, we transform our individual existence.

R.E.

PART One

The Need for Meditation

Self-Mastery 1

As long as a person is alive, he or she comes into contact with different things and beings and circumstances. Nobody in the world can, even for a moment, live without coming into contact with the objects of the world outside, or at least with his or her own thoughts and ideas.

Thus, not by choice, but by the compelling law of life, every one of us must meet our world of circumstances at every moment of life. If we are efficient in meeting our own world—if we have ready dexterity, decisiveness, firm will, balance, equanimity, and right understanding—no situation in life can break or enslave us. But unfortunately many among us succumb to the apparent threats of life's situations and become shattered personalities.

Despair amid Abundance

A tragedy seems to be confronting much of the world today. Young people, their heads stuffed with facts and figures, go about in the world weighed down with sorrow and desperation. They try to run away from an inner sense of dejection by loudly proclaiming the glories of their age and of the civilization of their times. The organs of propaganda noisily howl the glories of the machine-age, the high standard of living, the efficiency of financial transactions, the nobility of governments, and the glories of war that uphold the blessings of peace!

Wherever you turn, from morning till night, you hear pedantic acclamations of the present age—through the radio, the press, through journals and books, on the screen, in theaters, on public platforms, in houses of parliament, at international conferences, and even from the pulpit. But, despite all these exaggerated glori-fications, it is indeed a fact that every intelligent person with sensitive observation would readily conclude that there is obvi-ously more unhappiness today than ever before. Unless one is blind, one cannot mistake the sorrows etched on the face of human-ity in our times. The moment we take an honest look, we see desperation and tears.

I am not one of those who decry science and scientific inven-tions or the utility and efficiency of new methods of mechanical production or of modern systems of transport. Certainly science has discovered means and methods by which the drudgery of life has been almost lifted from our day-to-day existence. The necessi-ties of life, even luxury goods, have been brought within the reach of the lower middle class.

As a social being, the individual has to a large extent been redeemed from the slaveries of barbarous ages. A sort of primary literacy has come to bless more than half of humanity. The barriers of tribes have been broken asunder, and even the walls of national patriotism have been at many points broken down in order to enhance international brotherhood and friendship.

The people of one region of the globe wander to another for education, earning their livelihood almost at the antipodes of their birthplace, and their last remains rest in peace in yet a different quarter of the world. Thus, many people have become natives of the globe, beyond the fold of caste and creed, national prestige, or the dignities of blood-groups.

Yet, a superficial review of modern man in his "Brave New World" would provide melancholy reading. The pleasing surface of his world is like the painted beauty of a prostitute in the shaded streets at dusk, which under closer observation reveals the abhor-rence that often lies beneath it. What causes this painful illness in our life, which seems to be at best an ugly paradox when viewed against the glorious achievements of our era and its civilization?

The cause certainly cannot be any maladjustment in the outer world or any change in the behavior or construction of the world. The world of things remains more or less the same; and if there is any change in it, it is only for the better, because the human being with his advanced intellect has learned to tame wild nature. If the cause of our pain is not in the outer world—which we have successfully improved, in which we have harnessed into service

4

even the inert mineral world and have tickled unmanifest energies into manifestation, in which we have pressed every known energy and force to serve as loyal slaves—then we must inquire for the cause of sorrow in our own inner being.

When we thus enter into the inner world, no true critic of this age can, even for a moment, dare to compliment these times. Deep within ourselves, we have grown more barbarous than the barbarians who lived in the virgin jungles of the newborn world. We have become unconsciously cruel, selfish, and arrogant, and we often behave sadistically and hysterically. We have grown vulgar in our thoughts, low in our values, and shattered in our capacity to tackle our personal lives and its problems.

In short, the age has failed because we have lost our mastery over ourselves. In our preoccupation with conquering nature and subduing her to serve us, we have ignored our own inner monstrosities. We have developed the faculties of seeing with fleshy eyes and engaging all our abilities in setting right the things we have seen. We have left our subtler perceptions undeveloped, and, naturally, like a long-neglected garden, our inner world has grown into a jungle.

We live in the outer world, but prompted from our own within. Our character and personality determine the experiences that we gain in the outer world. Unless we learn to master our inner life, the outer scheme of life, however efficient and perfect, cannot but bring sorrow and unhappiness.

Unfortunately, this fundamental factor has been overlooked; and, as a result, in spite of prosperity, education and scholarship, and mastery over the outer world, the children of the modern age seem to make of their luxurious world a burial ground for all hope and joy. Their technological knowledge and efficient commerce provide them with a cross on which to hang their own individual peace. Their government and politics serve as two pillars across which runs the beam of national vanity; and along its length lie the dead carcasses of personal freedom, love, tolerance, and goodness. The vultures of deluded estimation feast upon this sad engine of death, self-created.

This image of a mourning parade of death, with carrions hooting and feeding upon goodness butchered, has become the insignia of our much-glorified materialism. If the wondrous philosophy of materialism has given us scientific progress on the one hand, it has also given us a glass of firewater with which to gulp down our sorrows. If it has given us modern government, it also has given us the unavoidable tragedy of marching to death to the tune of a national band twice in every generation! If materialism has saved us from our wars with nature, it has led us into the necessity of strangling, plundering, and looting our own fathers and children once in every quarter of a century. By the time the last generation returns home, disabled in body, perverted in mind, and confused in intellect, their irresponsible offspring, growing into the bloom of youth, have already been conscripted and forced to parade on the training grounds, armed to their teeth by the witches of science! Ridiculous is the paradox of this age.

Individually, no one in this generation glorifies any of the above or sanctions war or compliments immorality or gives his or her assent to hatred, lust, or murder. On the individual level, each admits that the atrocities committed nationally and communally are absurd and despicable, yet the very same criminalities become heroic and meritorious at the national level. In short, materialism has come to decay and death, convicted by its own law. We are now living through an age of agony that has become tired of its own self- created problems. The age is slowly sinking into a hopeless sense of utter despair, because it finds no way to regain its balance.

The present age has given us a long period of sorrow, and we have become addicted to misery. Like an opium addict, the melan- choly human being has come to believe that life without misery is putrefying death. He dreads bliss and peace. Misery and agitation have become natural to him; and modern man, though he sadly mourns his plight, dares not walk the path of self-mastery, but makes a new Bible of sorrow, an Upanishad of sighs, and a Koran of wretchedness.

I am neither a cynic nor a pessimist. I have only painted a realistic picture of the world we live in and the civilization we have built out of the spoils of our own confused intellect. The edifice of life stands bereft of the cement of love, haunted by the ghosts of despair and the devils of misery. Inside the chambers of this edifice, to sing the song of God has become the greatest blasphemy that one can perpetrate. One can find little hope that a new generation of evolved human beings, stable in their inward tranquillity, unshaken in their peace, divine in their noble perfections, can ever come to people the world as the children of these desperate fathers and mothers.

The Cure for Mental Anguish

When we turn to the great textbooks that explain the ancient rights of man, we find an exhaustive science of living by which it is possible to redeem even the worst among us. These textbooks are the scriptures of the world, and in all of them—whether they be the Upanishads of the Hindus, the Bible of the Christians, the Koran of the Muslims, the Dhammapada of the Buddhists, the Zend-Avesta of the Zoroastrians, or the Torah of the Jews—run the same threads of knowledge and technique by which the individual can be brought into harmony with Truth and be redeemed from his present cursedness to the divine heritage of his own inherent goodness.

The prophets and masters do not for a moment despair at even the worst type of individual. They seem to grow in their enthusiasm as they take in for treatment a subject with degraded, false values of life and wrong ways of living. Whoever the master and whatever his native language and the era in which he was born, the society to which he personally addresses his wisdom will always assert, "An individual who has mastered himself is a master of the external world."

The suffering of the present age, if diagnosed properly, will be found to be the result of man's own inward shattering. Each individual is a slave to his own passions. In his psychological weakness and intellectual impotence, he is incapacitated to control his passions and resist the suicidal temptations to strive to fulfill his sensuous impulses. Shattered between the wild forces of his uncontrolled personality, he becomes an inefficient instrument who cannot react to external challenges or intelligently digest his experiences in life. He finds no foothold for his personality. Like a dry leaf on a vast meadow, he becomes a victim of every passing breeze and gets tossed hither and thither aimlessly. This aimless tossing is the misery that characterizes our age.

If we train ourselves to live a life of self-mastery, that way of life is called *religion*. The technique is called *the good life* or *the divine life*, and the noble values of life pursued constitute *philosophy*. When we watch the world from this noble temple of religion, through every scripture-window in its walls, we see man being thwarted because he lacks self-mastery.

An individual who has mastered himself is a living institution in this world. The world exists to serve him. He alone is the inheritor of life. This self-mastery gives a person freedom from his

7

slavery to circumstances; no more does he come under the lashes of failures or sorrows. He, in his self-mastery, rises above the body into the noble heights of power and knowledge, worthy of becoming the king-of-kings, ever enjoying a peace and tranquillity deep within himself, which is impervious to even the greatest upheaval in the outer scheme of things.

The message of self-mastery is one and the same in all the scriptures of the world, though each scripture may teach a different technique of self-development. If these techniques were mastered, to whatever degree possible, by all the members of a generation, we could truly enjoy the godly blessing of the scientific age in which we live. Materialism is certainly acceptable and can be a blessing to us. The comforts of the scientific age, a life made easier by the use of machines, the profits gained by harnessing natural forces—all are ours by heritage. To decry them is to insult the intelligence of humanity. But when technology becomes our master and persecutes us, we must protest.

Foolish, indeed, is that scientist who creates a Frankenstein and in his intellectual vanity lets himself be haunted by the tyrant he created, refusing to destroy him. Unless the creator of Frankenstein can find a technique of developing himself to a greater strength than his creation, he has no right to protest against any member of society raising weapons to destroy this living threat.

Individually, each person has the right to rear a tiger in his house, but if it becomes wild and a threat to the community, the individual right is negated and the community justly demands the beast's destruction. Similarly, if humanity does not grow strong enough to become master of the machines it has created, this present civilization of slavery to iron wheels pounding to the rhythm of lust shall stand condemned. But should we develop a self-mastery potent enough to rule the forces of nature we have released, then certainly we shall preserve our secular endowments and come to live, served by them, as sultans of our destiny.

The technique of self-mastery expounded in all the great textbooks of true living advise us not to escape from life, but to maintain an intelligent way of living, according to our circumstances in life, and to use diligently and profitably all the inner and outer situations of our life. Religion is to be practiced not only in temples, prayer rooms, or hermitages. Religion, if it is to bless us with its joy, must be lived in the office, at home, and in the government chambers.

In every walk of life and at all moments, we must make use of the ever-changing pattern of challenges, and while consciously meeting them, we must train ourselves to become stronger individuals, with greater mastery over ourselves and the outer world. This diligent method of living consciously, struggling to better ourselves from moment to moment in our bodily strength, in our heart's emotions, and in our intellectual capacities, is the true religion, which transports even a base individual from the sorrows of a biped into the joys and perfections of a God-man.

The instrument with which we live through our experiences is not, as we think, the body. When we observe an individual, we see that the experiencer in him is not his body, but is in all instances his mental makeup and intellectual peculiarities. No doubt, his mind and intellect do come into contact with situations through the instrument of his body.[1] Thus in a given situation, the experience we gain is as much related to our body as a pair of glasses is related to the eyes. What the eyes see will be colored by the hue of the glasses; but the efficiency of vision depends entirely upon the efficacy of sight in the eyes. A blind person will see nothing through glasses. A color-blind person will see differently through green or blue glasses than a person of normal vision would. Obviously, therefore, the condition of the eyes is the primary factor in determining the clarity of the vision enjoyed.

Similarly, even though the experience of the world outside is gained through the body, the experiencer is, in fact, our mind-and-intellect equipment. A better vision of the external world is possible only when the imperfections of vision are removed. The imperfections of our experiences in the world outside can be fundamentally improved if the mind and intellect are disciplined to behave better in the face of all circumstances. Therefore, all techniques of self-improvement must be directed toward the disciplining and strengthening of the psychological and intellectual entities in us.

The methods of organized religions may have become enshrouded in exaggerated claims, in confusing descriptions, and in superstitious stupidities. Besides, the methods of orthodox

---

[1] Mind and intellect are here and throughout the book differentiated thus: mind is the aspect of thought characterized by doubt, emotions, and agitations; whereas intellect is the aspect of thought that judges, decides, and discriminates.

religions may require a restatement in the context of our times, for we find ourselves thrust into a world of unprecedented competition, where we are compelled to life a life of agitation, with impoverished mental stamina and twisted intellectual faculties.

Therefore, established religions often do not directly address us; and when we hear the call of religion, our minds fail to understand. But with a little conscious living for several months, strictly following physical, mental, and intellectual disciplines, anyone can come to a better understanding of his own religion.

I am addressing the followers of all religions who, in their enthusiasm, decry their respective religions and stand self-condemned. I will place before them the logic as well as the methods of meditation. Whoever assimilates the logic and begins his spiritual practice (*sādhanā*)² shall come to recognize the sanctity of all life and the true meaning of the religion of his birth. This is the first benefit, and there are a number of them, all finding their consummation in the glorious realization of the Divine.

---

² Consult the Glossary for the meanings of Sanskrit terms.

Meditation
and Life

2

A human being cannot rest contented without knowing. To know and understand seems to be the most virulent of our appetites. Thus, from the dawn of history we have been seeking to know, to understand, to investigate, and to discover greater fields of knowledge regarding the world of objects outside, as well as the world within. Knowledge of the world outside, constituted of things and beings perceived by our senses, forms the subject matter of science, while the inquiries pursued and the discoveries made in the world within, when codified into a systematic science of life, become philosophy.

Having discovered and understood the limitless number of objects and beings, science in her maturity turned her gaze toward an inquiry into the fundamental unit of matter. In the eighteenth and early nineteenth centuries, scientists discovered that the unit of matter was the atom and that there were something like ninety-two different elements in the world. In the twentieth century, the atom was discovered to be divisible, and the ultimate factor of matter was realized as energy.

Just as science has sought to discover the nature and behavior of things of the world, philosophy has been struggling, from the beginning of time, to discover the contents of the world within man. Therefore, to claim that philosophers are daydreamers, ineffectual poets, or utopian scholars would be to declare an ignorance of philosophy. Philosophers are striving to extend the kingdom of knowledge as much as the scientists are. The aim of the philosopher is as divine as that of the scientist; both are working to bring a greater happiness to mankind. The only essential difference between philosophers and scientists is the difference in their fields of inquiry.

The criticism that philosophy is impractical or that it has no direct bearing on life can to some extent be justified when one views the Western concept of philosophy. To the West, philosophy is essentially a *view of life*. The aim of philosophy in the West seems to be merely to envisage an ideal state of affairs and a goal of life to be achieved when the necessary conditions are created. The philosopher in the West sits comfortably in his armchair and, with the wrong end of his pen, points to a distant goal, thrilling and captivating in conception. Then he expects his readers to experience the possibilities of his perfected Heaven upon earth, purely in their imaginations.

In contrast to this is the philosophy of the Hindus, with its six main schools of thought, none of which are mere textbook descriptions of a utopian ideal. If philosophy had merely painted an ideal without providing the methods of working out its fulfillment, the practical-minded Aryans would have considered it poetry, not philosophy. They, in the Hindu tradition of thought, declared that philosophy should not only prescribe an ideal and a perfect view of life, but must also prescribe the means and methods by which everyone can reach that state of perfect living.

Thus, whereas in the West philosophy is merely a *view* of life, in the East it is, besides being a view of life, also a *way* of life. No Hindu school of philosophy has overlooked this aspect of the science of religion. Every one of them has a complete and clear prescription of a technique, following which the practitioner can be assured of achieving his or her spiritual goal. The practice of meditation is one such technique for reaching spiritual fulfillment.

From the very spirit of the Upanishads, the most profound among the philosophic writings of India, we can see that India's philosophers have been as much concerned with life as the physical scientists. The only difference between them is that while a scientist concerns himself with the life of objects, a philosopher concerns himself with life as such. In all spiritual and philosophic discussions in the Hindu tradition, we find a thoroughly rational and completely scientific investigation into the nature and composition of life and the factors that contribute to its harmony and disharmony.

* * *

Meditation has been glorified in the Hindu scriptures as the most sacred vocation of the human being. Humans alone are capable of this highest effort, by which they can hasten their own evolution and rise beyond the mind and intellect, the factors that limit them. Once an individual successfully transcends these limitations, he enters into the higher planes of perfection, pointed out by Darwin as the destiny of "the superman."

If we are simply advised to meditate, we will not be able to benefit from that advice since, as a generation, we are not ready to follow any advice unless it is based upon reason. Unless we know what meditation is, how are we to meditate? Thus, we require detailed explanation before we can understand exactly what the scriptures mean by prolonged meditation (*dhyāna*). The following chapters will serve that requirement.

Few of us can remain for a single moment without the mind and intellect roaming in clusters of thoughts. The question is: How can we control and regulate the production and flow of our thoughts? Only when we have developed a steady hold on our thoughts, and when we have gained mastery in controlling and directing their flow, can we say that we have become full-fledged human beings— or that we are capable of meditation.

The animal world, too, has a mind and intellect, though not fully developed. The human being is different from and superior to animals only through his capacity to integrate and develop, through conscious effort, both his mind and intellect. Once integrated, the vacillating mind comes under full control of the discriminating intellect.

When the mind gets thus chastened, the clarity and brilliance of that individual's intellect also come about. Thus each serves the other.[1] The cultivation of this control leads to the development of a fuller personality, and this marks the beginning of meditation.

---

[1] In fact, the mind and intellect are expressions of thoughts in two different functions: feeling (mind) and thinking (intellect).

The Basic Unit of Life 3

When the ancient rishis (seers who articulated the philosophic concepts known as Vedanta) brought the beams of their mighty intellects to observing, analyzing, and codifying their conclusions on life, they came upon rich and valuable discoveries that revealed the infinite possibilities and potentialities that lie dormant in every human being.

The contents of the scriptures cannot be considered an accidental production. They clearly indicate a slow-earned maturity in the field of thoughts and concepts. The rishis trained themselves to have the necessary detachment from life in order to observe it through the clear spectacles of logic and science. They never viewed life through the lens of prejudice or attachment. Each master passed on his observations to his disciples, who in turn observed their own generation; and if they had an original statement to make based on their own experience, they added it to the wisdom of their master. Thus, down through the centuries, an unbroken chain of human generations was closely observed by people of specialized inner discipline in order to determine the workings of life.

According to the rishis, every person is a potential genius. Beneath every sinner, they discovered a sage who is but waiting for redemption and recovery. This self-development and self-rediscovery is accomplished through the technique called meditation.

Life is a continuous process, with a set purpose, a glorious pattern, and a rigid logic. The life of each one of us is an effect that must have an independent cause, even though the cause may not be perceptible to us. Our present life is one of the innumerable incidents in our eternal existence. Even the prophets of science in the West have stumbled onto this truth. Darwin visualized a generation of supermen as a climax to the evolutionary process. So also the rishis of the Upanishads, long before Darwin, held that life is to be lived for the purpose of improving ourselves to reach the state of supermanhood.

When the great masters were closely observing life, they first investigated the basic constituent or unit of life—an experience. Their final declaration on life reads in the form of a definition: "Life is a series of continuous and unbroken experiences of objects." Just as the physical scientists, having discovered that the fundamental unit of matter is the atom, did not declare that science had fulfilled itself, but continued observing and analyzing the very atom, so also the great masters of old did not take to passive retirement after realizing that the unit of life is an experience, but diligently pursued their investigations to discover the modes and factors governing and controlling individual experiences. These investigations brought the great subjective thinkers to the truth that an experience is possible only when three essential factors come to play simultaneously in a given field—the subject, who is the *experiencer*; the object, which is the *experienced*; and the relationship between the subject and the object, which is the *experiencing*. They also discovered that an experience depends entirely upon the condition and the nature of these three factors.

In the absence of the subject, no knowledge of the object is possible. The object may be present, but if the subject is absent, the object cannot produce any knowledge or experience by itself. If somebody comes into your room while you are sleeping, the experience of having met the intruder is not yours because you, the subject, were absent from the field, although the intruder, the object, was in the room. You will also find that unless an established relationship exists between the subject and object in a given field, no experience is possible. For example, when you are fully immersed in a novel, you may not experience a visitor's arrival in your room.

Thus it becomes evident that an experience is the product of the experiencer, the experienced, and the experiencing, when all three come to play in a given field of time and space. If these be the factors of an experience, a study of life as such, which is a series of experiences, cannot be complete unless we thoroughly investigate the nature of these three distinct factors. In the light of this reasoning it must become clear that physical science is insufficient for bringing about our total redemption from the thralldom of our suffering, for science deals mainly with only one of the factors, the experienced—that is, with the world of objects.

The masters of the scriptures came to the conclusion that a scientific analysis of the subject and a diligent attempt at understanding it are the only methods sufficiently comprehensive in estimating life and planning the means and methods by which we may ultimately transform life's discordant notes into harmonious and divine music. Educated in the modern spirit, we are not in a position to appreciate this secret, and we hastily condemn the ancient thinkers for seemingly neglecting life and its activities in favor of adjusting, regulating, and controlling the inner personality.

In fact, a spiritual seeker sitting motionless with eyes closed in deep meditation is contributing to life as much as the politician on the public platform and the scientist in the laboratory. Science strives to bring about happiness to the community by reordering and readjusting things and patterns constituting the world around us. Spirituality strives to bring about a world of perfection through individual perfection; through spiritual values, religion readjusts and revolutionizes individual personalities in the community. Science in its inquiry is mainly extrovert and believes that happiness can be brought into our lives from the world outside. Philosophy is mainly introvert in its inquiry and believes that true happiness can only be brought into our lives from the world within.

Evidently, then, the accent in philosophical inquiry and spiritual pursuit must necessarily be upon the factors of the human personality, their constitution, and their individual and collective behaviors. No doubt the individual personality is to some extent under the influence of external circumstances and objects; but this dependence upon the outer world is maximum in plant life, and we observe that as the beings step higher upon the ladder of evolution, there is a corresponding release from slavish dependence upon circumstances. The more evolved a being, the more is he capable of outwitting or conquering his external circumstances. Naturally, therefore, the superman reaching his evolutionary fulfillment must necessarily be a master of all circumstances and a true ruler of the world within and without.

Spirit Enveloped in Matter

4

For the superman to emerge out from a frail mortal of endless limitations, a scientifically complete and philosophically true investigation into the subject is unavoidable. We find the clearest and most extensive inquiries into this subject in the philosophy of Vedanta. On the basis of their observations, the rishis declared that each one of us is not merely a physical structure, but every person is also a four-forked entity containing within himself four distinct personalities: the physical, the mental, the intellectual, and the spiritual.

Our Multiple Personalities

A man is seen strolling in the park clothed in an overcoat, sweater, shirt, and trousers, but none of these envelopments is the man himself. They are nothing but garments used for protecting him or for manifesting his personality or status. Similarly, when a philosophical mind views the naked man, it discovers that the individual consists of several layers of matter enveloping the core, the spirit. The rishis concluded that man is nothing but the spirit enveloped in matter. When life, clothed in layers of matter, walks out fully dressed to face the wintry weather of plurality and sorrows, there stands a human being.

The modern world, in all its activities—domestic, communal, social, national, or international—is at best feeling its way through the immediate darkness to reach wider fields of greater darkness when the government planners draft manifestoes of human rights under the false conclusion that each individual is but a mere physical structure. Materialism served by science can come only to the conclusion that more food and clothing, better shelter, more leisure and entertainment, and probably a little more education

17

will ensure happiness for everyone. In short, people are considered not much different from mute animals who are aware only of their body existence. But if we, along with the rishis, analyze the human being into three personalities *in addition* to his body existence, we can find out how these four personalities act and react with each other, and how they can be developed and integrated through the process of divine contemplation and devoted meditation. The theory of the spirituo-physical structure of man as propounded by the Vedantic seers is shown diagrammatically on page 20.

Undeniably, a mere physical body will not move or act unless the Life Principle is found enshrined in it. A dead body can no longer smile, eat, walk, think, or feel. No sooner has life flown out of it than the body falls down and starts decomposing into the very elements of which it had been formed. Thus, the Life Center in each one of us is the sacred spot from which all activities emanate. Without that Life Factor vitalizing the body, the mind, and the intellect, you would be nothing but inert matter unable to read, analyze, and understand these words.

This divine spark of life, this spiritual center, is called *Ātman* in Vedanta and is considered to be enveloped by layers of matter of varying degrees of grossness. The outermost shell, the grossest, is the body; and almost all through our conscious existence we go about considering ourselves to be only this body. Only a rare few become completely aware of the existence of their mental and intellectual selves, and fewer yet are those who are even remotely conscious of the *Ātman* within.

A controversy is raging among modern thinkers as to whether the mind is inert matter, or nonmatter having full consciousness. Upon this, a satirist has pronounced the judgment: "It does not matter if mind is matter," and, "Never mind if mind is not matter." All schools of philosophy in India accept that the mind is made up of subtle matter and that the body is constituted of gross matter. The Life Principle (*Ātman*) presides over both.

Ātman is represented in the diagram by the sacred symbol *Om*, ॐ. This is our Self, our real nature—omnipotent and omniscient. This *Ātman* has come to be enveloped, in a sense, by various matter envelopments called *sheaths*. No contact exists between these matter envelopments and *Ātman*, but the sheaths gain a semblance of life because of the presence of *Ātman*.

The diagram shows that there are five distinct sheaths: the *food sheath*, which is outermost; the *vital-air sheath* lining it; the *mental sheath* further within; the *intellectual sheath* still more interior; and lastly, the innermost, the most subtle of all the five, the *bliss sheath.*

When we say that one sheath is interior to the other, we mean that the inner one is subtler than the outer. The subtlety of a sheath is measured by its pervasiveness. For example, the size of a piece of ice is definite and measurable; but when melted, the water spreads over a larger area. Hence, in philosophical language, water is described as "subtler" than ice. If we boil the water, the steam formed will spread further than water. Therefore, steam, in a philosophical sense, is considered "subtler" than water. Similarly, the physical body is the grossest. The vital air we inhale can be blown out to fill a greater space than that occupied by the body. Thus, the vital-air sheath is subtler than the food sheath. Our mind (our feelings and emotions) can reach distant places where our breath cannot reach, and our intellect can visualize places that our mind cannot. For these reasons, we consider the mental sheath and the intellectual sheath subtler. The most subtle of all is *Ātman*: It envelops all and none envelops It; It is all-pervading, declare the Upanishads.

The composition of the various sheaths is as follows:

Food Sheath. The physical body of which everyone is fully aware during the waking state of consciousness is called the food sheath. It is born of food assimilated by the parents, it exists because of the food regularly taken in, and ultimately, after death, it must decompose to become food again. The physical structure, which arises from food, exists in food, and goes back to food, is most appropriately called the food sheath. The organs-of-knowledge (eyes, ears, nose, tongue, and skin) and the organs-of-action (hands, legs, organ of speech, genital organ, and organ of evacuation) exist in this sheath.

Vital-Air Sheath. The air we breathe mixes with our blood and reaches every cell of our physical body. Oxygen forms an inner lining, as it were, for the outer physical sheath. The vital-air sheath controls all the organs of action, and it is five-fold, with five different functions: (1) the faculty of perception (*prāṇa*), which controls the perceptions of the five sense organs; (2) the faculty of excretion (*apāna*), which controls the throwing out by the body of various things, such as spit, seeds, feces, urine, or perspiration; (3) the faculty of digestion (*samāna*), which controls digestion of food; (4) the faculty of circulation (*vyāna*), which controls the distribution of digested food to all parts of the body; and (5) the faculty of

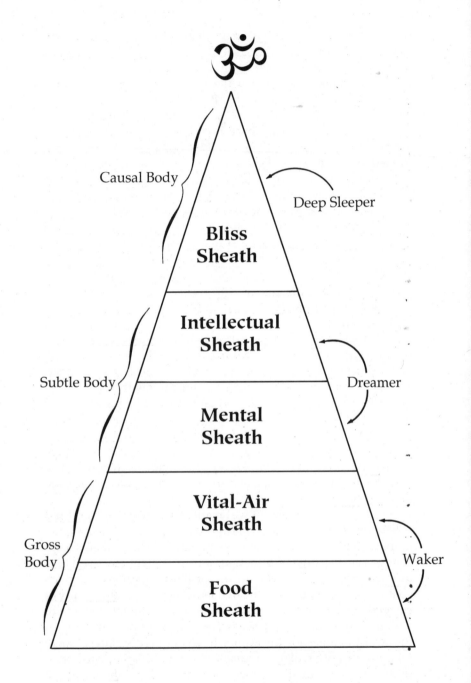

thinking (*udāna*), which makes it possible for people to entertain, absorb, and assimilate thoughts. The food and vital-air sheaths together are called the *gross body*.

Mental Sheath. None of us is unaware of the existence of the mind. The mind entertains our doubts, joys, and a variety of emotions, and constantly erupts with a nonstop flow of thought-lava. The mind can fly to things and places seen or heard, and because of its vast reaches, it is considered subtler than the food sheath and the vital-air sheath.

Intellectual Sheath. While the mind is the doubting element, the intellect is the determining factor in each of us. In Vedantic literature, the two are considered one and the same. When our thoughts arrive at a determined decision or a willed judgment, they are called the intellect. The intellect is subtler than the mind because it ventures forth into realms unheard and unseen. Realms not yet experienced are the fields of its revelry and conquest. The mind and intellect together are known as the *subtle body*.

Bliss Sheath. This, the subtlest of the sheaths, is made up of the ignorance (nonapprehension) that exists during our deep-sleep state of consciousness. It is considered blissful because, whatever be the condition of our waking consciousness, when once we fall asleep, whether rich or poor, successful or disappointed, healthy or sick, young or old, we experience undisturbed peace and bliss. We experience a state of pure nonapprehension, that is, the absence of everything. This sheath is called the *causal body*: from non-apprehension all the misapprehensions of the gross and subtle body arise.

Ātman, the Life Center, the subtlest of all, is the core of this five-sheathed structure. All these together constitute the spirituo-physical entity that plays as you and me. Consciousness exhibited by the organism depends upon the condition of its mental and intellectual sheaths. Stones have no awareness because the mind and intellect are absent in them. According to Vedanta, plants have a rudimentary mind and intellect, and hence they live and grow and possess some awareness. The minds and intellects of animals are further developed, and they are more aware than plants. The supreme development is reached in the human being.

The purer the mind and intellect, the brighter are the beams of consciousness that radiate from the individual. The saint or prophet is he who has the maximum awareness manifest in him.

"Brahmavit brahmaiva bhavati"—"the Knower of the Absolute becomes the Absolute," roar the Upanishads. To realize pure Awareness, which is *Ātman*, or the Life Center, is the goal of life, the culmination of evolution, the fulfillment of supermanhood.

The Hydra-Headed Monster

In reality, we are ever this Life Center, but, having fallen into an inexplicable misunderstanding, we identify ourselves with one or another of our outer envelopments (sheaths) and believe ourselves to be the corresponding individualities.[1] Thus, at one moment we are the body, as when we say, "I am short"; at another moment we are the mind, as when we say, "I am doubtful" or "I am worried"; and yet at another moment we consider ourselves to be the intellect, as when we say, "I have an idea."

The world of the subject is ever dancing in confusion, seeking after a profusion of desires: one moment, we think ourselves to be a mere body searching for its comforts; now, we are a bundle of sentiments and emotions; at another moment, vibrant and dynamic, we follow an ideology that the intellect has dictated; and at some other rare moments, we crackle to break the shackles of life and conquer the realm of the spirit.

Each of the personalities demands its individual satisfaction and distinct values. That which is satisfactory to the physical body may not be acceptable to the psychological personality. You may like to eat a lot of sweets—certainly a craving of the mind. But the doctor who cares for your body may advise a smaller intake of sugar because of the diabetic condition of the physical person in you. Intellectually, you may have convictions that corruption is bad, but the mind, riddled with desires, may give you enough sentimental arguments to justify going after illicit gains. In each one of us there seems to be a multiheaded personality, each head demanding its own satisfaction and possessing its own tastes, standards, and values. Ordinary people attempt to gain a sense of complete happiness by acquiring, organizing, preserving, and playing with the sense objects of the world. However, as soon as one of the four personalities has found its happiness, the others

---

[1] The ego that arises in us when we identify ourselves with the gross body is called the waker; with the subtle body, the dreamer; and with the causal body, the deep sleeper.

22

revolt in dissatisfaction. Thus, the hydra-headed monster seeks happiness by drinking from a single cup, when there are four parched throats, each demanding a different beverage altogether.

Obviously, there is a crowd of personalities in each of us. When we identify with one or another of the envelopments, we come to suffer the consequent sense of limitation, sorrow, and unrest. In this sense, *samsāra*—the sorrow-ridden cycle of birth, death, and rebirth to which we are subject as long as we remain ignorant of our higher nature—is our own creation, and the responsibility for our sense of limitations is our own. In spite of the profusion of personalities within us, we are ready to sacrifice the outer for the satisfaction of the inner sheaths. A gangrenous wound in the forearm of a person will cause unremitting mental torture. A surgeon's advice that the arm be amputated is very readily accepted. The person allows his gross body to be chopped off to cure the pain and agitation in his mind. In another instance, when a religious or a political ideal takes possession of a person's intellect, she is ready to suffer great physical discomfort and even mental torture for the sake of her cherished convictions. Thus, when we identify with our intellect, for the satisfaction thereof, we are prepared to ignore the demands of all our grosser sheaths.

Therefore, it is easy to understand the great prophets and masters, who, after discovering their real nature to be nothing but the *Ātman*, cheerfully suffered mental pains and mortification of the flesh. Christ crucified could sincerely and magnanimously pray, "Father, forgive them; for they know not what they do." Mahatma Gandhi in our own time, collapsing with bullets in his chest, could still chant the name of God, "Ram, Ram."

The masters of the Upanishads declared that their observations on our multiple personalities need not dishearten us. Instead, these facts should encourage us to venture forth into a closer and more diligent observation of life. The rishis explained a method of self-effort by which we can dissociate ourselves from the false attachments and wrong identifications with the matter envelopments and rediscover ourselves to be in essence nothing but the eternally sweet spirit. The process by which this consummation can finally take place is meditation.

It is said that Alexander the Great, during his victorious march along the plains of India, met a great master of North India who cared not to do obeisance to him, a mere temporal victor. The saint was jailed. The next day Alexander went to the captive and, introducing himself as the victorious emperor, commanded him to ask for any boon. The saint, it is reported, looked scornfully into the monarch's face and, with the serenity born of true wisdom, replied, "You obstruct the sun's light; please move over a little. This is all the boon I ask of you."

Rediscovery of the Self does not only end all our confusions and our sense of imperfection, but it is an ascent into a state of supermanhood or Godhood. The Upanishadic seers dreamed of a people, everyone of them a superman, who would be masters of all circumstances and situations around and within them. We must attempt to make this dream come true. Let us offer our animal values of life as oblations to the fires of our discrimination. This is *jñāna yoga*, the way of the discriminating mind. Blind faith born of fear and thriving on ignorance is a veritable chain of slavery! Knowledge alone lends an edge and gives a positive direction to our spiritual quest.

The Nature
of Desire

5

Acquiring and spending we lay waste our powers. Each of us seeks the same goal; we all want unadulterated, unbroken, absolute joy and peace among the sense objects that constitute the world of our waking state. However, sense objects have but a false glitter of joy that soon fades away. And at the loss of joy, the worldly seeker strives on to multiply his capacity for purchasing more of those same fleeting joys.

In this struggle for earning and spending, we are driven from one desire to another by the eternal, universal urge to reach a state of perfection. We become exhausted, dejected, and disappointed amid the uproar of a thousand unsatisfied yearnings. Then one day we leave our physical sheath—the vehicle for enjoying our waking state. What a cruel end!

If peace and joy are the goal of every living being's day-to-day struggles, it is quite natural to ask, "What is peace?" We must realize that the question is not about any physical phenomenon outside, whose analysis might be facilitated by laboratory experiments and visual and factual representations. The question is a subjective inquiry into a state of satisfaction felt within, experienced by the individual with or without reference to the external circumstances of the visible world.

By peace is meant the mental condition as experienced by the individual, and recognized as such in the absolute sorrowless silence within. Therefore, an inquiry into peace can be conducted only by a person who has achieved some detachment from the outside world and who has learned to look within and observe the happenings of his various mental states.

Self-analysis and introspection are the very beginnings of a philosophical inquiry into self-perfection. This is the perfect means of achieving a true, vital, blissful life. So long as the values respected in life are those of indulgence and feeding of sensual demands, our attention turns outward, and the chaos within is not mended.

We will strive to understand these inner processes. These theories have been the vital experiences of spiritual masters and are indeed facts that have been tested and found to be solid truths by the one behind this pen.

Tracing the Course of One Desire

We know that in every one of us there are, at any given moment, a hundred desires simultaneously struggling for fulfillment. Those fortunate ones who attain seeming fulfillment of some desires will find that each fulfillment provides the breeding ground for a dozen other new desires, each attempting to complete the imperfections of the phantom joy achieved through the fulfillment of the earlier desires.

Let us analyze a desire and observe what happens. "If only I had a son" is the beginning of an unending chain of lifelong self-tortures. The man wishing for a son feels that all the available circumstances in his life do not serve his conception of complete joy and do not therefore give him that texture of joy and peace that is his demand of life. His solution slowly gets crystallized in his vague desire that "my son would complete my joy more fully." His desire is thus an unconscious effort on his part to have a fuller expression of himself.

One desire—the desire for a son—is but a localized disturbance in his mental lake. But a million ringlets of concentric disturbances always follow, and the widening ripples of thought come to crush upon the vast banks. The desire motivates an endless array of thoughts; thoughts thus motivated by each desire get projected out into the waking-state world, and among its sense objects they manifest as actions. Successful actions end in the acquisition of the desired fruit—the objectification of the subjective desire.

The desire for a son produces the agitating problem whether to marry or not, and if the decision is to marry, the question of "who" crops up. As though by magic, at each leisure moment a million castles-in-the-air spring up to paint in the void the would-be life of man and wife in intricate detail—beauty, comforts, conveniences, and more. The thoughts feed the original desire. The desire vitalizes each flimsy dream. In a short time the consequent chaos creates a hell, a roaring inferno within. And all this arises but from one desire!

The individual, tortured by his own thoughts, cannot keep himself contained for long. As his thoughts gain vitality from his desire, they soon make him their slave. When these thoughts find their expression, there happens the seeking, the meeting, the talk, the transaction, the procession, and the wedding! Mentally strained and physically exhausted, the fellow and his bride hurry through the usual processes to breed. The one desire for a son, which caused the inner whirlwind and consequent rush of activity, at last condemns him to the thorny fields of fatherhood: "My son! He has arrived!"

The deep joy of fatherhood is reached, but only for a fleeting moment. The joy is immediately followed by his constant run for the baby's formula and feeding bottle, for the doctor, the nurse, and the pharmacist. Soon the beleaguered father is shuttled between the toy shop and home, the theater, the bookshop, and the school. Every day that very source of joy, "my son, " provides the father with a hundred hopes, tremblings, plans, failures, disappointments, and sorrows.

One may be tempted to ask, "But at least in that sacred moment when he cried out, 'My son!' don't you think he had a taste of real joy?" Another may say, "If there is any joy content in sense objects, why not arrest the moment and prolong it to any desired length of time?" Let us patiently continue our inquiry, and we may come to discover the secret of permanent joy.

We observed how the desire for a son caused a storm of thoughts, how they manifested in the world outside as action, and how the desire for a son was finally objectified. Let us see what happens to the father when he knows that his desire for a son has been fulfilled, say, at the moment of the last rending cry of the mother and the first cry of the child, or when the small infant is first laid in the father's lap. The inner ripples of agitation suddenly settle down. The thought disturbances caused by the desire for a son sink down, and for a split moment the mental stuff in its liquid clearness reflects the glory within. But the next moment the state of peace is gone! A thousand new desires arise regarding the son and his comforts and the mother and her health, disturbing the mind that had been stilled for one blissful moment.

The mind is at once the breeding ground of desire, the dungheap of contending thoughts, and also the glorious castle of perfect joy. When the mind is stilled—when it ceases erupting its scorching lava of thoughts—peace is the subjective experience of the possessor of that thoughtless mind. Peace is joy. That is why in peaceful, dreamless sleep every living creature feels nothing but joy.

From what we have so far observed it can be inferred that the father's joy was not in the son, but in the particular condition within that the birth of the son occasioned. Thus, the source of joy is not in the external world of objects, but is deep within us; and whenever the mind is at perfect rest, we experience an effulgent flood of inner bliss.

The desire for objects creates disturbances that shatter our real nature of inner peace. The struggle and the urgency of the individual to fulfill his desires represent the urge of Truth to assert Itself. The spirit within is asserting its need to come back to its normal state of fullness. The tension in the bowstring is from the consistent pull on the stem of the bow to regain its straight nature. The tension and pain of life are the result of Truth's benign pull upon untruth.

When we have thus discovered that desire breeds thoughts, that thoughts propel us to actions, and that when actions end in successful fruition, the thought-storm is calmed, producing a feeling of joy and peace—when we have discovered this chain of events, the solution for life's sorrows becomes self-evident. Renounce desire: thoughts will end. When the desire agitations are hushed, eternal peace is experienced. This experiencing of full satisfaction and contentment is independent of the external world and the day-to-day circumstances created around the subject by the world of objects. It is a perfect and achievable goal of life.

World Perfection through Self-Perfection

Having fully, intensely, and vividly lived this desireless state of bliss in his own experience, the liberated one (jīvanmukta) no longer responds to the world and its fleeting, illusory joys. Through all experiences and all pairs of opposites—joy or sorrow, honor or dishonor, peace or war, health or disease, heat or cold—the mahatma, the God-like individual, is ever well poised and lives on as an immortal among us mortals. "I alone AM," "I am full"—so sings the saint, immersed in peace as he sits upon his simple seat wrapped in a glorious feeling of absolute bliss, the supreme state of fulfillment.

You too can become one who, even while living in the body in this world, has gained perfect freedom from the endless demands of the body, mind, and intellect. Live intelligently. Be introverted. The outer world will still be as it is. History tells of the endless repetition of social, political, and international crises, and how each generation has thought, in the immediate living of its crises, that theirs was a time unparalleled.

Within a given fixed arc the pendulum of life moves between peace and war. It is a losing game to dedicate one's life to bringing about a perfect readjustment of the world. At best, a mere patchwork job can be done by individual effort. To herald in an era of peace, we have to help every human being live the enduring spiritual values of renunciation, desirelessness, nonattachment, and true understanding, which requires a universal program of blessing an entire generation with Vedantic education.

Let the world wait. It has endured long and has lived through much more horrid circumstances. We may safely conclude, therefore, that it will ever remain so. Let each one try his best to complete his own self-education. When a hundred persons come forward to live and experience Truth, *staying where they are*, then those hundred will become the invisible team for uplifting the world. Their spiritual dynamism is the only answer for the material challenge of atomic and hydrogen bombs.

Please do not misunderstand: I am not suggesting that we should be without sympathy for the present world. These words are written in deepest sympathy for our sorrowful world and its deplorable values.

Change the unhealthy values of lust, greed, selfishness, and extroverted desires. Live the glorious, life-giving, permanent values of love, charity, tolerance, introvertedness, and meditation. All is then done. The individual, shedding his mortal weakness, rises in his essential nature, to the state of Godhood.

This is an intimate experience sought out and actually experienced by perfected beings, not a utopian theory spun out of mere fancy. When you have carefully read and pondered upon the above, take the decision to test the truth of this pregnant slogan of the scriptures: "World perfection through self-perfection."

Spiritual Growth

6

Nothing for nothing. This is true everywhere—in the spiritual world no less than in the material. Plenty and prosperity have to be paid for with sweat and toil. In spiritual growth, there can be no progress without steady and sincere practice (*sādhanā*).

One begins to yearn for the supreme Truth only after one has sufficiently lived through experiences of joy and sorrow. In repeated births, an individualized ego (*jīva*) gathers definite sets of day-to-day experiences. In each of these embodiments, the *jīva*, confused by his own ignorance, strives and struggles to earn and spend, accept and reject, possess and give up, embrace and spurn. In this struggle, when a thousand mad hopes and pains of the *jīva* are still waiting in vain for their fulfillment, one day the body comes to the end of its course. It is mourned by dear and near ones. However, all the tears and funeral wreaths are unable to bring it back to life. It decays and is resolved into the elements from which it came.

In such repeated births and short, uncertain spans of existence, living through numberless vain hopes, unfulfilled desires, incomplete joys, thankless tasks, and unrewarded loves, the *jīva* slowly develops toward a stage of higher thinking and is confronted by soul-searching questions: What is life? Why was I born? What is life's aim? Is there no perfection to be achieved in life? Is life an impotent duration of barren struggles between two points—birth and death? Here we have a mortal who has evolved through the required lower lives and has come to the gate that opens to the fields of a divine life. Only after passing through the dingy caves of self-arrogating, egoistic acts can the *jīva* emerge into the open expanse of selfless love (*prema*). To break the shackles of our selfish cruelties and desire-prompted meanness is in itself the regaining of our native freedom and contentment, leading, in due time, to a recognition of the essential oneness of all creation.

The path is doubtless rugged, but only in the early stretches. The journey ends in a brilliant realization of love, tolerance, satisfaction, perfect equilibrium, and abiding peace.

The Divine versus the Worldly Life

Spiritual life does not have to be pursued in thick forests or lonely caves, nor is it only for certain extraordinary individuals of special qualifications. It is not achieved by running away from the world or living a beggarly life of idleness in some remote Himalayan valley. The votary of Truth need not change his clothes or apply some marks to his or her body, or for hours stand upon his head in the blazing sun. Shaving the head, keeping a begging bowl, throwing away all clothes, sitting on a bed of nails, or sleeping on lion-skins—these external changes have no real meaning, nor are they by themselves a true sign of a freed soul. Spiritual life is not dependent, except to a very negligible extent, on the place where you live, on the clothes you wear, on how you stand, or on the condition of the hair upon your head. There is only one way of attaining a divine life—by *living* a divine life.

Worldly life is a continuous experiencing of limitations, pains, and sorrows, now and then uplifted by a false, intoxicating waft of fleeting joy gained from some sense object. Spiritual life is a continuous attempt to live a divine life, with a full realization of its scope and values. The aspirant is now and then encouraged by fleeting glimpses of the real, dynamic bliss—God.

The aspirant's goal is an eternal experience. The individualized ego realizes his ultimate fulfillment in his merging with the existence-knowledge-bliss (*sat-cit-ānanda*) that Truth is. It is the supreme be-ness, the goal, the end. In that state of perfection, there is nothing that he does not have: there all desires are fulfilled. He is no more under the tyranny of his mortal limitations. Beyond time, space, and causality, beyond death and disease, above hopes and desires, he finds himself "The All." This is not a becoming—he merely regains his true nature by an intuitive "re-cognition" of the Self.

Hidden in the mass of rock, and visible only to the transcending vision of the sculptor, is the graceful form of the sculptor's creation. Only an artist can bring this hidden beauty out of a common piece of rock. He has the subtle intuition to see the glory and perfection of the form within. His attention is fixed upon this beauty, imperceptible to the ordinary eye, and he strips the rock of the gross portions that conceal the beauty within. At last it is done; the finished product emerges in all its perfection. The artist has added nothing of his own to bring about or heighten the beauty. The beauty was always throbbing in the secret womb of the rock; the sculptor only released it from the encircling mass of formless rock.

Man does not realize how gross he looks as he lives his worldly life, his eyes ever ready to overflow with tears from the smart of suffering. His brow is ploughed with discontent and perpetually sweating with exertions as he fights his own individual imperfections. And yet, the eternal Self, the beauty of beauties, God, the omnipotent and omniscient, lies deep within him, shrouded by layers of ignorance. To remove this veiling is to secure nearness to God, to "re-cognize" his essential nature, the Godhood.

The worldly life is led in agony and sorrow by a deluded *jīva* distorted by his ever-present dread of a continually threatening calamity—death. The divine life is experienced in joy and bliss, ever resplendent with life-giving wisdom, through which the *jīva* again finds his own essential Godhood. The divine life is the chiseling process by which Truth is brought out to fulfill Itself. In living the divine life, one realizes the Truth.

Divine life is the technique of self-perfection. To strive for the Truth is the highest of all conscious efforts of a human being. No other sentient being in the universe has the equipment for thus hastening its own evolution as efficiently as we can. If we with our wealth of available apparatus do not learn to spend our life in striving for perfection, ours, indeed, is a life wasted.

Every action of an individual in the outer world is but an attempt to express himself more fully. Every yearning and strife, every desire and effort, every thought and word is an unconscious effort to regain his state of fullness. But the trouble is that the phenomenal world of finite things and beings is not the field for seeking the Infinite, and so the worldly person never obtains the satisfaction that he daily seeks. The eternal Infinite alone is capable of satisfying him. Lasting satisfaction can never be reached by sense gratification.

The Infinite is our true nature. We have only to *realize* this— and we would find ourselves at our journey's end. All worldly actions, in an individual or in the aggregate, among men, animals, or plants, have the same motive—to escape pain and achieve bliss. Every movement, physical or mental, in every being—from the suckling child to the international warring heads of state, from the dog in the drawing room to the roaring lion in African forests, from the tiniest fungus to the giant oaks—is directed toward getting rid of pain and gaining happiness.

So universal is this instinctive dread of pain that even great thinkers have missed the mark and failed to read its obvious message. In this *revolt against pain* lies the clear declaration that bliss alone is Truth and that bliss alone is the real, eternal nature of the universe.

The true nature of the ocean is water; the waves, the foam, the sparkling ripples, and the flickering bubbles are all merely its various names and forms, having no separate individuality in themselves. So too, the multiplicity of things and beings observed in the universe is merely so many different names and forms of one and the same thing. In essence, the multifarious names and forms are all the same essential One, whose nature is bliss.

God is bliss. God resides in everything and everyone. To consider yourself as a separate individual, a Mr. Smith or Mrs. Jones, is as foolish as for each billowing wave to consider itself separate from the ocean. Because of this belief of separateness, the *jīva* is born. It is the *jīva* who suffers. The Mr. Smith or Mrs. Jones is the mortal, bound by his or her wishes and desires, tortured by pains and sorrows.

Choke the "I-ness" in you, and you will have already taken a substantial step toward freeing yourself from your bondage and realizing the fullness of your true stature: "Bliss am I," "Immortal am I," "God am I."

This "re-cognition" of the self is the crowning victory of life. This is *Īśvara darśana*, the "vision of God." Thereafter, the outer worldly circumstances of sorrow or joy, insult or respect, failure or success, heat or cold, fasting or feasting, hate or love, poverty or riches, disaster or progress cannot touch the liberated one. He is above all circumstances. He is no more a victim of the external, but is rooted in the wisdom of his inner essence. He becomes a calm witness of the universe, as though it were a mere temporary disturbance within him. Such an individual in his perfection becomes the superhuman saint. All powers, all knowledge, and all capabilities are his. His is the perfect bliss, which nothing can ever shake or even cloud. He lives out the fixed span of his life, blessing the world with his mere presence. Such a *jivanmukta* alone can truly serve, guide, and lead the world.

The Technique of Self-Perfection

You too can achieve this supreme state of endless bliss. How long will you waste your precious life in vainly seeking the Infinite among the finite sense objects? Stop your blind search. When your lost key is in your pocket, how can you find it anywhere else? Stop being easily excited. Forget disappointments. Compose yourself. For once search your own pocket.

Life is a search. With effort and consequent discovery, all pains will end. The rishis of India will lead the way. They ask of you only to be wholly sincere. Have an honest determination to be persevering and faithful. When the pain created by desires is removed, what remains is your essential nature, bliss. This bliss is in you, ever sanctifying and illuminating the outer world and the inner processes. It is this essence, the Self, the *Ātman* in this writer, that makes it possible for him to guide his pen. It is the Self in you that makes it possible for your eyes to see this writing, for your mind to register impressions as words and sentences, and for your intellect to determine their significance. Your intellectual understanding and the various ideas, doubts, disturbances, determinations, and emotions that rise up while you read these lines are, at this very moment, illuminated by the very same Self within you.

When you wear your Sunday suit, it moves and behaves just as the wearer. When the same suit is off the back of the wearer and is hanging on its hanger, it has no movement. The suit is dead when its master, the wearer, is not within its folds, vitalizing, directing, and determining its movement. Similar is the case with the physical body. As long as the wearer, the Lord, is within, the limbs move and the outer and inner organs function. To give this moving physical body an identity and a name and to arrogate to it an independent existence is in no way wiser than to claim a personality for the Sunday suit!

The physical body, with its organs-of-action and organs-of-perception, its physiological equipment and its psychological and intellectual processes, is the particular suit-of-the-day that the Self has chosen to wear. The mortal *jiva* is he who in his delusion has mistaken his suit to be himself!

You are not the body; you are the essence, the Self (*Ātman*), the divine entity within. Identify yourself with the finite body and you are a mortal; identify yourself with the Self, and you are an immortal.

When we identify with the body, the dream-giant ego manifests itself—often lust-filled, ever passionate, and constantly torn between a thousand contrary feelings, desires, and hopes. The ego alone suffers pain, limitations, and finally death. In identifying with the Self, the phantom ego disappears, and in its place we recognize the divine Godhood, peaceful and contented, with nothing to desire or to wish for—our true nature. The attempts to disassociate ourselves from our identification with the body and the consistent practice of seeking our real identity in the Self constitute the divine life. It can be pursued through any one of four paths: *jñāna yoga* (path of knowledge), *rāja yoga* (asceticism), *bhakti yoga* (path of devotion), or *karma yoga* (path of selfless action).[1]

Sādhanā is a practice that is followed regularly so that we may learn to live a spiritual life. It is a sacred self-effort (*puruṣārtha*). We can make or remake our future. The present is not the tyrannical dispensation of a power-mad, superhuman dictator, God. It was made by each of us, for ourselves, in our past hours, days, and lives. Our self-effort in the past is our destiny in the present. So then the *puruṣārtha* of the present will be the destiny of the future. Make your tomorrow peaceful by living today in right understanding, divine thought, and selfless action.

Thoughts are creative. Each wish of ours must find itself fulfilled in time. Out of the bundle of wishes we had in the past, a certain set has come to bear fulfillment now. The aggregate of these fulfillments and experiences during a fixed period in time and in a limited concept of space is what we call life.

A wish expressed in mental language is a thought. If there are no wishes, no thoughts arise, nor can wishes ever germinate when thoughts have stopped their flow. Renounce all your desires, and your thoughts cease. Arrest your flow of thoughts by bringing your attention to the single idea of your goal. With either method the mind can be annihilated. The life lived in pursuit of this total annihilation of the mind is the divine life.

---

[1] See Chapter 15 for an elaboration on *jñāna*, *bhakti*, and *karma yogas*.

Thoughts in their incessant flow create the substantial fiction of the monstrous-looking inner instrument called the mind. In this thought-castle, behind its cardboard walls of memory, hope, self-ishness, and pride, sits the doll-king, "I," a phantom tyrant, who, self-centered and sensuous, rules over a fantasy kingdom of sorrow. Stop thought and the thought-castle crumbles down over the doll-king, "I."

The Life Divine is the Kingdom of God. "Thy Kingdom come" is a state antecedent to "my ego-bound kingdom go." "Thy King-dom" is in reality my own. Not realizing this, I suffer. To realize this, the supreme wisdom, is the experience in *samadhi*, the blissful state of transcendence of the body, mind, and intellect. This rediscovery of oneself, for oneself, is the culmination of all right effort, the supreme *purusartha*, which leads us away from all our pains, limitations, ignorance, and darkness to bliss, peace, wisdom, and light.

Live the divine life wherever you are. You need not give up your position in life, your business, your family, or your possessions. A slight change in your outlook is all that is required. Simply abandon the attitude "I, Mr. Jones, desire or plan to execute," which will naturally fortify in you the feeling of "I-ness." Have a spirit of dedication to the Lord and roam happily through life in the safe and true belief that "He is the Truth. His will alone be done. May I be ever an instrument in His hands, and through this body may His plans be fulfilled." When a person effects total elimination of his egocentric dross, he becomes a God upon earth. His is all love, all success, all joy. His is wisdom absolute. The questions that confronted him as he gradually grew away from worldly passions trouble him no more.

While still seeking, he hesitated in doubt and asked, "What is life?" Now he knows that existence as "I" is a long eternity of pain, and that true life can be only an eternal experiencing of the Life Divine, when the frail mortal breaks his fetters to rise up as a God-man. "Why was I born?" was another question that haunted him before the final moment of liberation. Now he knows the answer: "I was born only to wake up and assert my true nature, which is wisdom and bliss."

Along with his growing sense of dissatisfaction, even with the best that worldly life can give, the aspirant, in his earlier stages, finds himself asking: "What is the aim of life? Is there not a perfection to be achieved? Is life a mere interval of sighs and smiles between birth and death?" Today in his wisdom he has the clue to the riddle. He declares, "Life is to seek and to discover Truth! Truth is perfection. As long as perfection is not realized as one's own self, the man-worm lives in a dungheap. When the divine, eternal principle of Self is realized, out of the worm springs the Lord of Lords, the ruler of bliss—God."

A liberated person lies dormant in every mortal. As butter is in milk, God is in you. Soured milk is curd; churn the curd and you have butter. When the external life of sense objects has lost its charm, the "curd" is ready for churning. Divine life churns your life of imperfections and brings up for you the butter, the essence—Truth. Live the divine life and enter the Life Divine, where you will have perfect joy and eternal satisfaction. Live the worldly life and know snatches of joy, fleeting glimpses of satisfaction, and countless hours of suffering. This is the choice. May your choice be eternal happiness.

1 An object supposed to possess occult powers & worn as an amulet or charm

How to Begin

7.

The most common question asked by new aspirants is, "How can I start living the divine life?" The question is quite natural and ought to be the logical inquiry one's mind makes when one has decided to walk the path of Truth. But when each inquiry is taken by itself in relation to the problem as a whole, the question to be answered seems to ask for and expect some ·miraculous secret talisman¹which, by a mere touch, would hasten one's spiritual growth. There is no such secret charm.

The divine life is a systematic way of living certain noble· values of the head and the heart. It is a steady process of renouncing the negative values of the material life now being lived and of accepting the vows of the right, positive values of the divine life. This revolution in one's thinking constitutes the impulses for the divine life. There is no secret magic by which even the greatest of gurus can, by a mere look, touch, thought, or word, get his disciples established in spirituality.

The child learns to walk by walking and falling and walking again. The youth learns to swim by swimming and sinking and swimming again. So too in the divine life; and therefore there can be only one answer to the question, "How can I start living the divine life?" Start by starting! The divine life will be yours when you live it despite frequent falls. Start to live it again after each such fall.

The child as it learns to walk has parents nearby to help; the girl learning to ride a bicycle has a brother or sister or friend at hand to help her learn balance; the youth has other swimmers close by to help him each time he sinks. In your attempt to live the divine life, your guru, be he far or near, will each time save you from the aftereffects of such falls and encourage you to continue the sacred pilgrimage toward Godhood.

Introspection and Self-Analysis

We have examined the life now lived by you as though you were an unattached spectator. Under this observation, the worldly life of earning and spending, of desires and disappointments, of love and hate, of "I-ness" and "my-ness" was stripped of its glittering, alluring aspects. You have decided to walk out of its embrace.

We can impartially judge something only when we stand apart from it. Detachment cannot exist when we have a sense of intense ownership or possessiveness. That is why an author or an artist consults reviewers for their opinions. Our attachments lend a false beauty to things; blinded with the pride of possession, we often fail to see the ugliness of cherished possessions.

Just as we, blinded by attachments and prejudices, fail to see the real nature of things and beings, so also do we, deluded by our lack of detachment, remain blissfully ignorant of our own weaknesses and faults. The divine life starts with the practice of detaching ourselves from our body, mind, and intellect, and impartially estimating the motives, intentions, and purposes that lie behind our thoughts, words, and deeds.

Such impartial witnessing is called *introspection*. It is no easy feat to accomplish. Self-analysis and self-criticism are hard and relentless tasks. At every stage our self-conceit and egoistic self-congratulation cover our faults and shortcomings and invest them with a false charm. No one can easily understand himself as he is, though he may be an intelligent and acute critic of other people and their actions, of institutions and their achievements; yet, in himself, he may be harboring a million weaknesses and faults, often the very same he so honestly condemns in others! This contradiction exists because, even for the best of us, it is a trial and a severe challenge to be asked to observe ourselves.

Each person generally goes about with the idea that he or she has an ideal personality. Very few of us are without some kind of a conception of what is the ideal. The very attributes of the ideal—honesty, goodness, love, selflessness, tolerance, pleasantness, and cheerfulness—create in our thoughts a total ideal personality; and, in our eagerness to be that ideal, we accept ourselves as actually established in that ideal already. Only others around us know how far away we are from the goal!

No one approximates his own idea of the ideal. This mistake is often seen in elderly seekers and in the majority of neophyte monks. In fact, they behave, think, and feel differently from how they *believe* they are behaving, thinking, and feeling.

In the contrast between what we actually are and what we believe ourselves to be is the first great hurdle we need to overcome as aspirants. Introspection, or self-analysis, is the only means to relieve this initial block. Self-evaluation is the only method of learning to know ourselves. Regular practice in detaching one's ego from oneself and watching it with pure, impartial judgment is introspection.

Invariably self-examination reveals negative values, false hopes, self-polluting thoughts, low passions, animal urges, and impossible dreams. In short, our inner life contains a good deal of Mr. Hyde: conceit, delusion, endless arrogance, laughable stupidities, and reprehensible brutalities. To apprehend this creature within is to discover a creature who fights, loots, kills, earns, hoards, acquires, and multiplies—all to delude himself with some impermanent and incomplete satisfaction.

It is difficult to apprehend the devils lurking within. Though most may be detected, an insignificant few may still remain to grin and cut a grotesque caper. But if the aspirant has the will, courage, and confidence in his own strength, he can apprehend them all. He who has honesty of purpose, and the heroism to cleanse his mind of animalism by replacing negative worldly tendencies with positive divine principles, is the true inheritor of the Life Divine.

From what has been said it may seem that introspection is impossibly difficult and unpleasant. But it is not. Within a few days you will realize that it is a simple and amusing occupation, at once entertaining and profitable. When some of your personal weaknesses—jealousy, lust, anger, selfishness—are apprehended, and some effort has been made in negating them with the opposite divine qualities of love, confidence, serenity, equanimity, largeheartedness, and selflessness, you will quickly find that you feel happier than before. Unconsciously you begin spreading cheer. These are the early fruits of studying your personality and improving it to a point that compels attention and respect.

The best time to introspect is at the close of the day's activities. After dinner a restful repose floods the mind. Anxieties for the morrow refuse to rise up with the usual din and roar. The disappointments of the day do not disturb the after-dinner peace. This is the sacred hour for negation and assertion; the psychological person in you is, at this moment, receptive and vividly transparent. In this quiet half hour let your mind rest in its impartial seat of judgment. Let the day's activities, actions, motives, thoughts, and feelings stream by. What you earlier believed to have been an honest show of charity on your part may now reveal itself as selfishly motivated. Your offering to help a fatherless child's education may now be exposed as a move to gain the attention of the charming young widow. An afternoon quarrel with your friend, on principles, may be found to have arisen purely from your wounded vanity. Your vehement condemnation of religion to the club members may be revealed as an escape from the consciousness of your own imperfections or an expression of ignorance of your own religion.

During your after-dinner rest, you can examine the entire day and watch yourself alternately playing the villain and the hero in the drama of your just-spent day. The observer in you becomes ashamed of the false actor within. This realization of yourself as you are is *alone* sufficient to effect an immediate improvement in your personality. Wrong values will drop off, and new, noble values will begin to thrive. You must not suffer consciously any known blemish in your personality. Animalism thrives on your ignorance. Detect it—and the next moment it is routed.

We bathe our body—we shampoo, powder, and beautify it; but we have neither the time nor the patience to attend to the messy condition of our inner personality. And at the same time we know that the character is the person. This is the most deplorable of neglects, a lamentable self-condemnation. Our failures are as much our own creations as are our successes.

Act Now

The vague idea "I must be happy" will not help better your present. Act! If you want to be happy, build the conditions necessary for real and substantial happiness. When the subject, the receiver, and the object, the giver, are both ready, the transaction will take place. The transaction is the experience. If an intelligent choice has been made, if the right subject comes upon the required object, the experience is happiness. If either of them is not in tune with the other, the result is sorrow.

You are not wrong if you think, "Is it as easy as that?" Why not? Should life be a perpetual struggle and an endless botheration—a vale of tears through which generations pass, weary and tired, ever seeking and never finding a resting place in which to lay away their burden of sorrows and relax? To many of us, suffering has become a habit, and even if we are told the way to bliss, we cannot accept it. After living a number of years in a cage, the parrot dreads its freedom and refuses to leave its prison even when the doors are left open!

The divine life is not for habitual pain-eaters. It is meant for the intelligent and heroic seeker who has come to realize that the life he lives within the tight cocoon of his desires, passions, and lusts is a worm-life of limitations. Original thinkers and sensitive temperaments alone can gain admission into the noble precincts of the divine life.

The quest for happiness is the one common thirst in all, be it in animal-life or plant-life. The very process of evolution is spurred on by the urge to be happy, ever motivating, encouraging, and guiding it. What is this quest? We want something and start striving for it only when we have a total absence of that thing in us, or when we have it in insufficient quantity. So then the quest for happiness indicates a feeling of its total or partial absence, and consists of our efforts to generate that experience. But do we know whether we can really create happiness as such?

Some people claim that, though direct manufacture of happiness may be impossible, it is, indeed, possible to manipulate external objects and circumstances into a favorable design that will yield a feeling of happiness. These are the successful people of the material world—rich, honored, and generally accepted as intelligent.

According to the materialists, happiness is a product enjoyed by the experiencer when he is with the object of desired experience, and is favorably disposed to rhyme with the given time, place, and thing. The materialists do admit that the experiencer will have different experiences with the same objects of experience—when they are arranged differently, or are made available at different times, or are brought into contact with the experiencer in different places. Your wife and children visiting your office while you are engrossed in work are a nuisance. The same is true when an overzealous host disturbs your midnight sleep to inquire if you would like to have a cup of tea. The problem of synchronizing the subject with its favored objects to produce happiness is difficult. It must be far more easy to balance a billiard ball on a knife's edge!

Hence life has become very complicated for us. The subject remaining the same, depending on the conditions of time and place, the very same objects provide different reactions. Nor does the subject remain stationary; he is an ever-changing entity, and with each disturbance in his physical, mental, or intellectual sheaths, he is a different personality with new demands.

It is rare that a subject contacts the right set of objects in a favorable relationship within a given time and place. And even if this unique chance presents itself, it cannot maintain its perfection for more than a fleeting interval, since the particular set of objects has nothing but chance and movement to guarantee any permanence.

We sweat and toil to bring the kaleidoscopic patterns of the ever-changing objects to a certain wished-for symmetry wherein we vainly hope to find happiness. Only when the wish of the moment is fulfilled will we discover that the quantity and quality of happiness we expected were not in the objects to give.

Thus, the poor envy the rich and wish to be rich. The rich look up to the king and wish they were the king. The king, seeing the cheerful cowherd, wishes, "If only I were so!" The childless yearn for children; the unmarried desire marriage; the married yearn for divorce! The judge is jealous of the doctor; and the doctor moans, "If only I were an engineer!" Each at the very peak of his material success comes to feel its hollowness, and the incompleteness of even the best that material life can offer.

The race was taxing, the journey long, the efforts great, the endurance heroic, yet the achievement is but an unsatisfactory, flavorless glitter of happiness. On closer inspection, the best of life's victories exposes imperfections, and we are hurled into another thousand attempts to experience joy. Thus, from desire to desire we are driven to seek and strive, never attaining what we actually want.

The Life Divine is life without problems, ills, or pains. It is the perfect life, where complete, eternal, all-perfect happiness is the experience. Since objects are ever-changing in time and place, how can we compel the required circumstances to remain eternally about us and provide us with a perfect life of happiness? "There is a method" is the unanimous assertion of the perfected souls, the rishis. The goal and the way to which they call us is Vedanta.

The attempt to live the life of Vedanta is the divine life. Its final achievement is absolute bliss, the Life Divine. The only path of progress for the imperfect is practice. Through divine life we can reach the Life Divine. Our daily attempts to review with detachment our life as lived during the day is the gateway to the right path.

Illusion
and Reality 8

The world we experience is an assortment of varied forms, names, tastes, smells, and sensations. These sense impulses are reported by our sense organs to the mind, which, in consultation with the intellect, forms certain opinions. These are arrived at generally by comparing the present experience with similar or dissimilar experiences in the past, the impressions of which were carefully stored away in our memory and labeled as good or bad, joyful or sorrowful, painful or pleasurable, loving or hateful. In the language of philosophy, these are called *the pairs* (*dvandvās*).

When the subject comes in contact with an object, it reacts to the encounter, and one of a variety of possible experiences is the result. The same object can provide greatly different experiences when the mood or condition of the subject is altered. That which was a pleasure in winter becomes a torture in summer. What was a joy in youth is a regret in old age. Peacetime literature condemns as a disgrace to civilization and an insult to the dignity of humankind those very actions that wartime literature extols as the duty of every honorable citizen.

The worldly person seeks joy amid the confusions of his own ever-changing moods and in frenzied efforts to match up his mood of the moment with the equally unpredictable changes in the objects around him. It is no wonder that he comes to grief. Not even the greatest of acrobats can maintain his equilibrium with two wild and unreined horses! The futile attempts to solve the ever-changing subject-object puzzle is the secret ulcer that condemns us to a life of agonizing pain.

The only permanent solution to the problem is to fix at least one side of the equation to a constant factor. The seeker, even during his early days of practice, through correct discrimination comes to the right understanding that the subject within who seems to experience the vicissitudes of life is a false entity and that an equally false world of objects dances a purposeless rhythm of change. The false subject is the conception of "I" as "Mr. So and So," which in actuality is a mere bundle of thoughts, the mind.

The subject-object puzzle remains a conundrum only to one who, in ignorance of the solution, dances vainly to keep in step with an ever-changing set of factors—multiple sense objects, fickle circumstances, endless desires and thirsts. Our failures and sufferings are due to defects in the methods by which we carry on the business of life. Once we accept the conclusion that pain and mortality are all for the mind (that is, for our sense of "I") and that sense objects can inject their venom of greed and passion only when the mind is tuned toward them, we have discovered the specific for the cancer of life.

The Illusory World

Had the waking world and its enchantments been eternally true and their effects absolute and real, then during our deep-sleep state we would have at least an inkling of their existence. As it is, no person can complain that he had no joy or peace during deep sleep. If he suffered while asleep, then he had no deep sleep that night, for no pain or regret enters the hall of deep slumber.

In deep sleep, when the mind ceases to function, where are the objects of the world, their charms, or their plurality? What happens then to the pain of bereavement or the joy of success? When the mind functions, the outer world flares up with its burden of imperfections, limitations, decay, and death. When the mind is at rest, the world dissolves into nothingness.

The great Vedantic philosophers brought to bear upon this line of inquiry their extraordinary analytical acumen and their vivid intuitional experience. They observed that in deep sleep even the most intimate of emotions and the deepest of memories are shut off from the sleeper's cognitive experience; and as the individual enters the plane of the waking state, there is a sudden bursting forth of memories and a multiplicity of sense experiences.

Our knowledge of our world of experience, which includes both outer sense objects and inner thoughts, and of the memories of such knowledge gained in the past, is indeed merely the tricky functioning of the mind. Where the mind is, the waking-state world (*jagat*) also is; where the mind is not, as in deep sleep, the world is not.

To gain freedom, we merely have to understand that our enemy is but an illusion of our own mind, and then train ourselves to calm down the dreadful emotions that our mental mistake caused!

Vedanta explains that the world in which we suffer has as much reality and capacity to give pain as the snake-bite which the wayfarer *thought* he experienced when he stepped on a harmless rope, mistaking it for a snake. The snake was but a mental illusion. The pains of the sufferer are indeed poignantly true for him. But the next passerby, after stepping on the same rope, goes on his way carefree and happy, because his flashlight illumined the rope for what it is. Naturally, it was not the rope that caused the pain for the first traveler. The pain was the result of his ignorance.

Only knowledge will remove ignorance. Deep and steady inquiry into the nature of the world, of God, and of the subject, "I," constitutes the enduring and noble pursuit of self-perfection. Perfection is achieved when the victor comes to live in eternal bliss— a destination which, once reached, completely removes all the phantom problems, ills, and pains of life.

We do not know that the objects we crave and toil to acquire have no more reality than the unreal snake met by the wayfarer. Objects and their capacities to give joy or pain are our own mental superimpositions. Since the mind is the instrument with which we cognize things that are not real in both our waking and dream states, the remedy lies in perfect control of the mind through consistent reeducation. The mind must be controlled in its freedom to roam among the sense objects seeking joy and satisfaction, and has to be reeducated to renounce its false desires, illusory fears and sorrows, and fancied joys. In short, the mind must be trained through correct thinking and diligent practice to recognize the world to be as unreal as the snake superimposed on the rope.

Inner War

If the mind is the "Satan" that has come to haunt our divine, blissful nature, no war is as sacred and as universal as the inner war for peace that each one of us wages in silence and devotion. Sector by sector everyone must win his own victories in the fields of thought. Mind, the fearful enemy, will prove to be nothing but a bundle of impressions created by thoughts of the past, which in turn create the thoughts of the present.

Can one desire or incessantly strive to possess a *dwadingole*? Certainly not. "Because," one would say, "I don't know what it is." Therefore, to think of a thing one must have either previous knowledge of it—meaning an experience of it—or must have at least heard of it. The thoughts that rise in us are solely about things or incidents previously experienced by the mind, through the physical senses; and they are amplifications or extensions of ideas or feelings already apprehended.

Thus, through the five sense organs, the mind experiences the outer world and gains impressions. These impressions (*vāsanās*) generate thoughts. Thoughts excite the sensory nerve-tips. To satisfy these physical itches, the human being, the roof and crown of things, labors, sweats, and toils, reaping a harvest of tears and regrets.

Control the licentious sense organs and the cause of the disease is arrested. Watch the mind and its modifications—the thoughts. When thought disturbances cease, the mind is no more a mint of sorrow.

The technique of training the mind to forget its haunting dream-visions of the world and to remember its native visions of Heaven is called meditation. Meditation alone can raise the individual to the largest common multiple so that he reacts uniformly to every changing scheme of time, place, and circumstance. Through regular and patient practice, meditation gains in steadiness and content. As it soars higher and higher, a new dynamic power of alertness is generated in the peaceful, thought-free hollow of the mind. At the peak of its eminence, the mind, thus packed with its own supercharged alertness, bursts into smithereens—all in a blinding flash of true wisdom: "I alone am." The world was but an illusion created by the unsteadied mind. There is only the One—the Truth.

In truth neither the meditator nor the meditated, and much less the meditation, exists. There is no subject, no object, no relationship. All dissolves into the One, which is but an eternal, vital experiencing. "Pure Existence am I," sings the person of wisdom (*jñānī*) in silent and motionless adoration of his own Self, which in Itself is the All. "I sought God," he roars from the heights of his experience, "and found Him in Me as Me. He am I. I am He."

This is our blissful goal, our eternal achievement. Soon after this voiceless experience (*samādhi*), the mortal rises from his seat of meditation a God indeed, immortal among men—immortal because he is no longer hooked to the pain-giving shocks of incessant change. In him the Vedas are accomplished. In him life is vindicated. In him is found the destination of all evolution.

A person of wisdom who has experienced God in himself thereafter knows no sorrow. His is an experience of endless bliss; his is an attitude of perfect detachment from life's fitful fevers. Even if his body be subject to phenomenal conditions of illness, which may strike a superficial observer as utter misery, the saint, living as he does entirely in his own inner nature of bliss, knows nothing but the ultimate joy of Godhood.

Sitting under a wayside tree, almost naked, his body shivering with cold, physically famished and probably sick, the mahatma (literally, "great soul") seems to present to the self-satisfied worldly person a tragic picture depicting melancholy wretchedness. He may consider the mahatma mad, while the mahatma, disturbed from his blissful experience of the Self by the noise of the rich man's car, may open his eyes and call out to the gathering crowd that it is they who are really mad, they who go about their lives like worms when each of them is really a king of kings.

But who cares for the words of a naked and starving Godman? If God Himself were to come right now, He would probably not even be offered a seat unless He wore a clean suit and pretended to be an agent of Messrs. Sin and Sorrow, Inc., the famous multibillion-dollar manufacturers of illusion and falsehood!

Character
Is the Man

9

A particular phonograph record plays a particular song because of the distinct pattern of etchings on it. The difference between two records, both of the same material, size, and shape, is the difference between the etchings on them. We may call a record good or bad, praise it or deprecate it, love it or hate it, all because of the etchings that guide the phonograph needle. The material of which the record is made deserves neither praise nor blame. It will take any pattern of etching the record manufacturer may choose to give it; a pleasant, lilting tune or a mere jarring noise, a moving lyric or loathsome rubbish, soul-stirring music or sensuous ribaldry may all be recorded with equal ease. Once recorded and fixed, the sounds become entombed, to be resurrected at will by the play of the needle. The etchings form the "character" of the record, its distinguishing feature.

Actions—Solidified Thoughts

People too have their distinguishing marks that determine their character. What are they? Certainly, there are many physical types, differing from one another in stature, girth, color, and features. Such differences, however, are differences in the mass of matter accumulation, like the differences between various vessels of clay used for storing water. A thickly set, robust man, a mountain of flesh and bones, may be a coward within; on the other hand, a lean, small-statured woman may be a gallant person. The real difference between the two is in their different reactions to the challenges of life. These differences constitute their distinguishing marks, their character.

Life brings forth laughter from some, but only sobs from others. Some feel submerged in the ocean of life, others keep afloat gracefully. Some take fright and would run away from life, others embrace it joyfully. For some people life is a burden, to others it is an opportunity. Some feel elated or depressed at discontinuous bits of life lived in meaningless patches, others sense a unity in its apparent diversities. For some life is an edifying song, for others it is profitless noise. How can these varied behaviors be accounted for?

Over our physical body reigns the mind. In the mind thoughts flow ceaselessly. In fact, the mind is defined as *a flow of thoughts*. As thoughts flow, they leave marks, or impressions, called *vāsanās*. Our behavior springs from this record of thoughts. The gross body merely obeys, or interprets into actions, the commands relayed from the mind. The body is merely an instrument of our thoughts. Actions are thus nothing but solidified thoughts. "As we think, so we become" is an old adage.

It is the difference in thoughts that distinguishes person from person. A distinct pattern of thoughts or of marks left by their flow forms a distinct and unique character. Beside the differences in human character, the differences between physical bodies have little significance. The body, the instrument of the mind, will not fail to reflect either the glory or the wretchedness of the mind. A profusion of thoughts lacking in intensity produces a weak, indistinct character. A strong character may cover the handicap of, and lend strength to, a weak and frail body; whereas a weak character may simply fail to harness the abilities of even a strong body. This does not, however, mean that physical culture should be neglected. A strong body is an asset *as far as it goes*, but a strong mind is surely a more valuable possession.

The ideal that suggests itself is a strong, healthy body presided over by a strong, healthy mind—a perfect harmony, a balance between the physical and the mental faculties, a relationship similar to that of a flute player and his flute. Without the flute player, the flute is a mere piece of hollow reed. It is the player who transforms it into an instrument of enchanting music. Don't pamper the body by doping the mind, nor court the mind, neglecting the body. Hand in glove they should move treading the path of Truth, a path of joyous fellowship between thought and action. And yet, the mind is greater than the body just as the flute player is greater than the flute.

We often hear of persons described as having little character. Such persons have no distinguishing mental traits—they have no definite *vāsanā*-chart to guide their course. They are mere straws drifting in life's current; they are without mental backbone or moral strength. Such persons are more or less at par with animals, who can be herded together and led toward good or evil.

Obviously, then, the way to influence a person is through his or her thoughts. This is where books, lectures, talks, and discussions play a key role in all efforts at self-perfection. Living examples, however, are more effective. That is how great saints and sages inspire us. By this method or that, or by all the methods combined, we can change our thought-flow pattern. The etchings on the mind change, and consequently the character changes. Character can, therefore, be changed at will, but the intellect has to demand this change. It has to break the wrong lines of thinking pursued by the mind and redirect the thoughts into the right channels. From animal-man we can change to man-man, and then evolve further into God-man.

If this globe of ours is to be made into a decent place to live, we have to cultivate in our character honor, truthfulness, fidelity, and love, and come to live a life of selfless self-respect. Only those people in whom self-respect is ingrained get through life unscathed by dishonor. By this leverage individuals can become high-minded and grow to become a nation's great sons and daughters.

Neither deadly slow nor tumultuous should be the flow of our thoughts. It should be smooth and steady, in tune with the Highest. It is the obvious duty of parents to inculcate high-mindedness in their children, and of spiritual teachers to lift them up to be people of sterling character.

It seems an idle platitude to say that when thoughts are changed, a person's character is totally transformed. Though the statement is true, in practice the seeker will find the changing of thoughts the most impracticable of all techniques. To change the existing pattern of thoughts is no easy accomplishment. In fact, the mind flowing in its usual channels will not be easily available for any change in direction. Although transformation of character is not easy, the great rishis, in their attempts at self-perfection, long ago discovered the subtle art of taming the mind. This secret alchemy of changing the baser person into an evolved being by the mysterious touch of scriptural knowledge is the *art of meditation*.

Making the Mind Pliable for Remolding

Ordinarily, the mind and its thoughts are stubborn and not avail-

able for remolding. If force is applied, the mind shatters into
smithereens like a crystal vase. However, if the vase is first heated,
it becomes pliable and can be remolded. Similarly, the stubborn
mind can also be rendered pliable for remolding. The heat in which
the inner personality gains the necessary pliability is the warmth of
reverence.

Most of us lack reverence toward religious matters. What we
generally understand as reverence is either a mere intellectual
appreciation or an emotional appeal for the spiritual ideal. Neither
constitutes reverence. When we come to appreciate an ideal intellectually and at the same time surrender our heart in love and
devotion, then we experience reverence. Thus, if appreciation and
respect belong to the intellect and if love and devotion are the
offerings of the heart, then reverence is the joint adoration of both
the head and the heart at one and the same altar. When a person
shows reverence toward an ideal, then he becomes that ideal: he
gains "at-onement" with the ideal.

Against this background, we can see the logic in the instruction of the rishis that every seeker, before entering into meditation,
must invoke a reverential attitude of total surrender and supreme
devotion to the guru. When our personality is in an attitude of
reverential dedication unto the Lord, or of surrender to the teacher,
our nature becomes available for recasting into a nobler mold.

The somewhat mechanical process of mentally conceiving
the form of the Lord, or of the teacher, cannot promise any reward.
After invoking the form, mentally prostrate and surrender the
ineffectual, self-centered ego, built on false vanity, flimsy wealth,
and impermanent relationships. Surrender with love, total dedication, and loyalty. Cry out for guidance, light, knowledge, and
strength. The mind will then become pliable enough to be remolded
into a new form of strength and beauty.

A sample of the attitude of the mind in total surrender might
be:

"O Lord, my beloved Teacher, here I am—tired and weary
from my labors to win happiness among the perishing objects of the
world. In ignorance I sought and gained much, but the temple of
joy crumbled before I could even lay its roof.

"I have nothing to offer except my own tears. I have nothing
to claim for myself except the fatigue of my indulgences, the stink
of my selfish acts, the sweat of my passions, and the cords of my
attachments. I have no right to demand even Your charity, for I

have never been charitable; nor to expect Your love, for I have never truly loved anyone. And yet, Lord, I am confident of Your infinite mercy. I surrender fully. Accept me as I am and mold me into a better shape.

"Guide me; lead me; show me the goal. Give me the strength to walk the path and reach the goal. My imperfections are many, but I yearn for You, my Lord—for Your help and Your companionship. Give me, Lord, a sure sign of Your grace and Your glory."

Or, from the Christian tradition:

"Almighty and most merciful Father, we have erred, and strayed from Thy ways like lost sheep. We have followed too much the devices and desires of our own hearts. We have offended against Thy holy laws. We have left undone those things that we ought to have done; and we have done those things that we ought not to have done; and there is no health in us. But Thou, O Lord, have mercy upon us, miserable offenders. Spare Thou those, O God, who confess their faults. Restore Thou those who are penitent, according to Thy promises declared unto mankind in Christ Jesus, our Lord. And grant, O most merciful Father, for His sake, that we may hereafter live a godly, righteous, and sober life, to the glory of Thy holy Name. Amen.[1]

---

[1] From the Daily Office of the Episcopal Church.

The Gross Body 10

A stone is unaware of the external world of circumstances. Plants are not aware of any inner world of thoughts; animals, though aware of the external world and the mental zone, are not conscious of their intellect. The human being is the only animal that is, to a comparatively greater degree, at once conscious of the world outside and the world within; that is, he is the only being who has developed the mental and intellectual faculties. The attempt of the seeker is to develop this awareness to such an extent that he or she becomes aware of not only the outer and the inner worlds, but also of the innermost spirit. The rishis, considering the human being as the one endowed with the greatest manifestation of awareness, closely analyzed the grades of consciousness through which he or she lives. They codified their exhaustive study and defined the three states of consciousness: the *waking* state, the *dream* state, and the *deep-sleep* state. The *Māṇḍūkya Upaniṣad* provides us with an exhaustive study of these three states and their comparative features.[1]

The rishis discovered that in each of these different planes of consciousness the individual identifies himself with a different layer of matter. Thus, with reference to these three states, they classified the five sheaths[2] into three distinct bodies.

---

[1] In Gaudapada's Gloss of the *Māṇḍūkya*, he uses in his discussion not only dialectics, syllogisms, and *reductio ad absurdum*, but also what is known in Western logic as analogical reasoning, so that through comparative study of the three states he may prove the illusoriness of the waking state on the grounds of its similarity to the world of dreams.

[2] Discussed in Chapter 4.

The *gross body*, consisting of the food and the vital-air sheaths, is the platform from which we look out into the world where sense objects are made available for our cognition. This state of consciousness is called the *waking state*. The mind and the intellect together constitute the *subtle body*, identifying with which we look into an inner world of experiences. This state is known as the *dream state*. When we have withdrawn from the waking state and have also folded up our dream world, we are in the *state of deep sleep*, in which we identify ourselves with the bliss sheath, called the *causal body* by the seers.

Beyond these three states extends the divine domain of Truth. So then ours should be an attempt to end consciously our false identification with the gross, the subtle, and the causal bodies. When we succeed in doing so, we shall rediscover ourselves to be the spiritual entity, the illuminating factor, the very Life Center in us. The Upanishads call this state *turīya*, meaning "the fourth." In discovering this state of God-consciousness, we discover ourselves to be that which is the changeless in all change, the permanent in all transitoriness, the eternal in the temporal.

Through meditation the seeker consciously withdraws his vigilant attention from the ordinary fields of dissipation, layer by layer. The first stage of preparation for meditation is a certain amount of withdrawal from the world of sense enjoyment and sense activities. Withdrawal is not suppression, but should be understood as steady sublimation. There is a difference between mental suppression and sublimation. Suppression is effected by a forceful self-denial based upon blind belief, untrained enthusiasm, or superstition. Sublimation, on the other hand, is the elimination of some of the false values of the mind as a result of intellectual understanding and conscious persuasion. Suppression degenerates an individual; sublimation unfolds in him a stronger, deeper personality.

We have already found that each one of us consists of multiple personalities, and that we judge the world of things and circumstances differently according to the particular personality functioning in us at a given moment.[3] That which we may accept as an ideal state of things from the standpoint of the physical being may not be acceptable to our psychological being. Thus, the picture of the

---

[3] See Chapter 4.

world and its happenings changes from moment to moment for the same observer.

In a materialistic era, the world is generally viewed from the standpoint of the physical person. The more we look at the world from the point of view of the body, the more we are lured by the seeming charms of a multitude of objects. The same world, to a Vedantic seeker, is imperfect and unacceptable because he views it through his intellect. Under his intellectual searchlight our world of compelling beauty reveals itself as ugly. Therefore, a student of Vedanta, eager to pursue the spiritual path of discrimination and meditation, finds himself instinctively withdrawing from the outer worldly life of sense objects, their illusory attractions, and his own panting pursuits after them.

The seeker on the Vedantic path has ordinarily the least concern for his body. He has the capacity to ignore the body, withdrawing from it and remaining intensely identified with the mind-intellect. To him, withdrawal of his attention from the body is easier than it is for an ordinary individual steeped in all-encompassing body consciousness.

Discrimination and correct thinking confirm the aspirant's conclusion that the body is a liability, goading him to endless exertions in satisfying its infinite demands. A student of Vedanta easily withdraws from the fields of sense objects, as well as from his preoccupation with body awareness and its attendant responsibilities.

However, we generally do not have that high a caliber of keen discrimination *(viveka)* and dispassion *(vairāgya)*. Especially in these days of nervous hurry and divided aims, it is difficult to live a life of discrimination all the hours of the day. We live instead half by instinct and half by training. Rarely, if at all, do we know how to think and live independently. Originality in life is condemned in modern society, for these are the days when imitative repetition seems to be the fashion. But the techniques that were effective in the past for developing one's discriminative capacity will be equally effective even today. The methods of self-perfection visualized in the various religions of the world are eternal in their application, and the most fundamental of them is meditation.

The Subtle Body

11

As you withdraw your attention from external sense objects through the technique of complete and conscious relaxation, your attention, to a large extent, withdraws even from your physical body. The more you relax, the more you withdraw your attention from the physical structure. Even when relaxation is not total, you will experience joy and peace.

The only method of eliminating a problem is to rise above it. No problem can be solved if we remain within it. A problem is created because of a field of circumstances. Unless we can get away from that field, the problem cannot be solved. The problem of our attention being dissipated through body consciousness can be solved only when we get away from that problem. In the *Bhagavad Gītā* this technique is elaborately discussed by Lord Krishna.

Getting away from the field of the body is achieved by consciously entering the mental and the intellectual zones. When you are deeply agitated you are the least conscious of the body. Even the most luxury-loving person on the eve of his election to public office will function splendidly in heat and cold and readily undergo severe physical privations. In his enthusiasm to win the election, he lives more and more intensely in his mental and intellectual fields and ignores the usual comforts of his physical entity.

Engage yourself more and more intensely in your mental and intellectual fields, and you will learn consciously to withdraw your attention from your physical body. Meditation upon the Lord's form and repetition of His name (*japa*)[1] are techniques by which the spiritual seeker becomes more and more fixed in his subtle body

---

[1] *Japa* is discussed in detail in Chapter 16.

(the mind and intellect) and thus experiences oblivion, at least for the time being, to the body and its surroundings.

Vedantic texts consider the subtle body to function in four different aspects. First, the subtle body is called the *mind* when it operates in the field of doubts and feelings. But when the subtle body functions as the firm, discriminating, and determining factor, it is the *intellect*, the second aspect of the subtle body.

Unless the doubts, and the determined judgments that act upon these doubts, are illumined for us, they cannot be experienced. Yet we all know our thoughts, and we see that from moment to moment we make judgments on every mental issue. The illuminating aspect in the mental zone that makes our thoughts apparent to us is the third aspect of the subtle body (*citta*).

Even if the thoughts and the intellectual decisions are illumined, they cannot give us a comprehensive experience of the whole unless they have a bond of synthesis. In our day-to-day experiences we have that sense of oneness when we realize that *our* doubts have been cleared by *our* intellect. For example, a friend has a problem but lacks the intellectual poise to reach a decision. We hear of his doubts and come to a decision that is reasonable and wise. Yet we cannot say that the friend will experience the consolation of finding a solution to his problem. Unless he has the egocentric attitude that the doubt is *his* and the final solution is also *his*, he cannot experience the totality of the inner life as every intelligent thinking person should.

Since every one of us is conscious of our status as a thinking individual, we can presume that there is in us a common denominator underlying both our thoughts and our decisions. This common denominator is vanity, and is expressed as "my thoughts" and "my decisions." When the subtle body functions as this sense of "I-ness" and "my-ness," it is designated as the *ego*.

Thus, the subtle body functions on four different levels and has four different names according to the field in which it is functioning. Whether he is father to a son, husband to a wife, or officer, friend, or foe in relationship with different individuals, a man remains always himself. Similarly, in spite of all these different functions of the subtle body, the individual is one and the same.

With this preliminary knowledge of the structure and functions of the subtle body, we can learn to understand how to engage ourselves in the subtle body to the exclusion of the physical structure and its world. The methods advised by the great religions of the world all help us to live more fully in our mental and intellectual sheaths. A direct approach to the mental zone is through the path of devotion, *bhakti yoga*. The clearest and the most direct technique by which one can come to live intensively and consciously in the intellectual sheath and transcend it is called the path of knowledge, *jñāna yoga*. The logic behind these two techniques is the same, since to control the mind is to control the intellect, both being one and same.

If your nature is predominately emotional, you can learn to surrender your ego at the feet of the Lord through the path of devotion. A devoted mind finds consummation when it is totally engaged in thoughts about God and not distracted by sense objects. At that moment of concentration, the devotee is totally unaware of the external world and withdraws his attention from his physical body. When the mind entertains a solitary thought as inspiring as that of the Lord, it often disappears in sacred sublimation, followed by an inexplicable but complete fusion with that which lies beyond the mind—the Self.

The final goal is the same when the intellect, through philosophical contemplation, reaches the maximum heights of thought. There, by the sheer magnificence of the prospects, the intellect renounces all its flutterings and composes itself into a tranquil stillness full of awareness. An intellect thus made still is an intellect that has been transcended. And, as with the mind, beyond the intellect lies the eternal Truth, the Self.

To say that the mind is transcended or destroyed is to say that the intellect, the *citta*, or the ego has been transcended. To declare that the intellect has been crossed over is to say that the mind has been stilled or that the ego has been annihilated. The transcendence of one is the transcendence of all. The process of meditation is the process by which the mind is stopped, the intellect transcended, the ego crushed, or the *citta* liquidated.

When this knowledge is translated into practice, one gradually becomes established in the subtle body. Seekers wanting to live the life of meditation must seek a program of activity in the meditation seat that will establish them more firmly in the subtle and gain the necessary withdrawal from the gross.

Once we can, by any process, reach the subtle and get established in it, we will find that we have solved our problems concerning the world and the body. Our problems then shall be of the subtle body only.

Why Meditate? *12*

Think of a person who takes one step forward and the next step backward, the third step toward his right, and the fourth to the left. In which direction do you think he would progress?

He reaches nowhere, even though such mutually canceling efforts be repeated *ad infinitum*. The only advice that can be given to such a person is that he resolve his conflicts and make up his mind as to the direction he means to follow. With nothing to pull him back nor to sidetrack his progress, he is sure to reach the chosen destination.

The need for integrating the various conflicting aspects of our personality is obvious. Our physical, mental, intellectual, and spiritual personalities must be blended into one harmonious whole. Meditation is the technique for achieving this harmony. It is the highest spiritual discipline. Through meditation we come to experience peace within ourselves. Internecine wars between desires end. Conflicts between duties no longer torment us. The mind is able to view life as a whole. Meaningless flutterings and consequent dissipations stop. We now can direct our potentialities with increased concentration that can no longer be shattered.

No one will have failed to notice the result of concentration among natural phenomena or in human activities. The sun's rays converged on a point through a focusing lens will burn the object on which they are concentrated. Successful people in business and in the professions owe their successes to single-pointed efforts. Application of a divided mind brings about indifferent results. The scriptures have rightly emphasized that every person is a potential genius. Most of us are able to use only an insignificant part of our infinite potentialities; therefore, disappointments are our inevitable lot. We have unlimited powers which, unfortunately, we have not learned to tap and make use of. It is a question of rediscovering ourselves. Beneath all our superficialities lurks a constant unconscious search for the common denominator. Along a single trail at one and the same time move all the different aspects of our personality—in order to reach the common destination, the experience of Reality.

The mind flutters from one object to another. The flow of thoughts is ceaseless. Obviously, before the mind can be made to concentrate on anything, it must be cultivated. In meditation the mind is made to withdraw its attention from sense objects. The intellect, asserting its mastery over the mind, orders it to stop all thoughts except the thought of the common denominator. By assiduous practice the mind learns to think of only one thing at a time. Such a mind is a force to be reckoned with; it actually becomes invincible.

Having become conscious of its true nature, such a mind is not disturbed either by passing sorrows or ephemeral worldly joys. Prosperity cannot spoil it, nor can adversity degrade it. Just as the scientific discovery of the indestructibility of matter and energy gives new meaning to objects, realization of *sat-cit-ānanda* (existence-knowledge-bliss) by the mind-intellect, through meditation, gives a new edge to life, stripping all worldly shows of their power to delude. All curtains lift before the penetrating gaze of a mind thus established in pure Consciousness through regular meditation. Shorn of all complexes, it is no longer assailed by any doubts or fears.

Start meditation now, and soon the incomparable experience of the gifts it showers on you will obviate mere logic.

The Process of
Meditation

Prepare
for Meditation *13*

In preparing ourselves for meditation, we should first acquire the ability to look within. We have been shooting our attention outward. We are vaguely aware, if at all, of the inner mental world. Just as a child requires training, a newborn aspirant must learn to recognize the world within, and then learn to walk among the sense objects of the world.

Watch the Mind

You must learn to go about your daily routine and uninterruptedly watch the mind. Each thought, word, and deed should emerge from you bearing the seal of your own recognition. Post a portion of your attention as a sentry in the watchtower within—the intellect. Let it be a silent observer of the workings of your inner life and estimate the motives, intentions, and purposes that lie behind your thoughts, words, and deeds. In addition, practice introspection at the close of each day.[1] Order a parade of the day's incidents, thoughts, words, actions, emotions, and reactions for your impartial review.

In the beginning the attempts at self-analysis may prove to be unsatisfactory. Your first analysis may seem like the narration of the ideal life lived by a god! Nevertheless, continue the practice. Seek to discover weaknesses, faults, and animalisms in each day's transactions. This process is called *detection*. Within a week it will be revealed that yours is not, in any sense, a god's life. Such dark reports should not discourage you. The darker the reports, the greater should be your effort to readjust your values and redirect your thought currents. Inner reformation always comes with revelation. When you have detected the weaknesses and are

---

[1] Explained in Chapter 7.

ashamed of them, at that moment those traits are dead. This stage is known as _negation._

At this point, you have won only half the battle. In the wake of each victory comes the onerous task of constructive peace. As soon as you apprehend and defeat a weakness, substitute its opposite virtue in your personality. Thereafter, look for its play during each day's dealings, and you will find how the new virtue grows to be a natural trait in you. This stage is called _substitution._

Introspection, detection, negation, and substitution—these constitute the preliminary processes in the purification and tempering of the seeker. Without this mellowing treatment, one is not fit for the strains of spiritual growth. Neglect of this unavoidable preparation for divine life has landed many enthusiasts on the wastelands of despair. Many have this common complaint: "I have been a seeker for years, and yet I have found neither the peace nor the joy that the scriptures promise." If the mirror's surface is oily, the face reflected in it is oily. Any amount of effort to clean the face is of no avail so long as the mirror remains unclean. Thus, it is not the fault of the spiritual texts if their promises are not fulfilled in a seeker, for unless he undergoes the entire preliminary purification process, progress will inevitably be hampered.

"Liquids find their level" is a proved scientific truth; yet water in two separate vessels need not seek to establish the same level. It is a necessary condition that the containers be connected together; then alone this scientific truth comes into play. Unless he establishes his contact with God, no divinity can flow into the seeker. Contact is a condition in the fulfillment of which spiritual growth comes into play. This contact is established by living the divine life. Even then the potential divinity cannot flood the mind of the person trying to live the divine life if he is already too full of the undivine. "Empty thyself, and I shall fill thee" is an eternal promise. This emptying of undivine contents starts with introspection, and is effected through careful, consistent detection and negation of the grosser animal instincts. Substitution is the secret of invoking divine grace.

One who thus starts his practice with diligent daily introspection ensures himself against melancholy feelings of futility and failure. Even those who are now on the path and are face to face with the dark and dreadful feeling of "Lord! I have wasted so many years of devoted endeavor!" must at once start self-analysis. In a few weeks' time, the seeker will have to confess that he is smoothly sailing forward as never before. And introspection will certainly accelerate the speed of progress in those who are already well on their way toward their life's goal. Therefore, introspect daily. Detect diligently. Negate ruthlessly. Substitute wisely. Grow steadily. And be happy, free, and immortal. Be a God-man.

Develop a Devotional Attitude

Before entering into meditation, it is necessary to pray. Meditation is a contemplative flight. Contemplation is not mere intellection or sheer emotional sentimentalism. Contemplative flight is sustained only when we come to spread in full both our head and heart as wings to keep our balance during this inward pilgrimage. Therefore, we must have confidence in a protecting power that guides and sustains our subtle efforts in this unknown field, and thus every seeker is advised first to invoke the blessings of the Lord of his heart. Your prophet, your Lord, or your guru can be the deity in your worship. There is absolute freedom for you to conceive of the Supreme through any symbolism you choose. Symbolism cannot be avoided, for at this stage of development we live in the plane of the mind. The mind cannot conceive of the formless Infinite.

The guru, for the purposes of meditation, is one who has guided you to detect and experience your divinity. He need not be a priest or a monk; he can be a friend, a leader in society, or an insignificant person in your neighborhood. He who has through his life and work unveiled a greater vision, provided you with a thirst to aspire, or kindled in you a greater hunger to live and to face your problems courageously—he is your guru. The teacher may be a book, it may be a passing statement, it may be an experience in life itself. The teacher is the one whose remembrance helps you to become a critic of yourself. He is a guide who, at all moments of moral and ethical compromises, rises up somewhere in your memory to warn you not to fall prey to temptations, and lends you courage to come away from the fascination of the moment and walk heroically the rugged path of righteousness.

Posture

In the face of a man approaching us we can easily detect whether he is cheerful or miserable. There is something in the lines of his face that clearly declares his mental attitude. So too, you can never express love or devotion with your sleeves rolled up and your fists clenched tight. It is equally true that in a kneeling position on the ground, with your hands upstretched and your face upturned, you cannot express ideas of vengeance, cruelty, murder, or hate.

Not only does your mental condition advertise its nature upon the physical body, but the position and condition of the physical body, to a large extent, determine and control your mental attitude. There is a close relationship between physical posture and mental condition. This relationship was clearly understood by India's ancient sages. They averred that for prayer or meditation, a conducive physical posture would be a great blessing. After years of experimenting they concluded that a developed student could meditate in any pose and in any condition, but that for the novice a special physical meditative posture would be necessary to induce a devotional mood and help arrest the roaming of the mind.

The posture recommended is that you sit on a flat cushion or folded blanket with your maximum base firmly on the seat, the vertical column erect and perpendicular to the ground. There is no regulation as to how the legs should rest. Most important is that you keep the legs in a position that offers minimum strain. Folding the legs has a physiological effect, for in that position the least amount of blood will flow to the lower half of the body, thus making a larger amount of blood available for the capillaries of the brain. During meditation the intellect has to function intensely, and this intense functioning is probably facilitated when a larger amount of blood is made available for the brain.

A bent or strained vertebral column interferes with the functioning of the nervous system and helps to disintegrate feelings and thoughts; hence the necessity for keeping the vertebral column perpendicular to the base. If the body is kept erect over its base, it will be in equilibrium, with its center of gravity contained in the base.

Thought-Massage

Experienced masters advise that the meditator next relax the body in the elected position. We are always straining and stiffening thousands of muscles, keeping ourselves stiff during the day and while we sleep. It is rare that we achieve complete relaxation. Relaxation of the muscles revitalizes the cells. Wondrous cures for even incurable diseases can be achieved if we know the trick of consciously relaxing the particular limb or organ that needs rejuvenation. Relaxation before meditation is effected through a process called *thought-massage*, by which the meditator, with closed eyes, sends his thoughts consciously down his body, mentally massaging and relaxing every muscle.

Starting with the neck, will that your muscles be completely relaxed. Then come down to your shoulders, and having relaxed the shoulder muscles, let your thoughts inspect the chest and the belly muscles. Roaming about the body, inspecting every area, your thoughts wander around the side muscles, the back, the thighs, the lower legs, and the feet down to the tips of your toes; also your upper arm, lower arm, palm, and fingers. Experience will show you that such relaxed arms can be most comfortably rested if the hands are laid in the lap with the fingers of the right hand interlocked with those of the left. When the body is relaxed, you will find that you feel heavier against the seat, or that the seat presses upward with increased insistence.

In this position of relaxation, you put off the physical body, as it were, upon a cross represented by the erect vertebral column and the collarbones. Just as one hangs one's coat on a coat-hanger, you feel your body being carefully removed and hung on your shoulders. The gross weight and tensions of the body no longer pull your attention to the physical plane. You have entered the meditation seat, with all the preliminaries of body adjustment completed.

The strength of meditation does not depend upon the kind of seat you use. You can meditate even in bed, on a sofa, or atop a stone wall, under any condition or in any position—*once you have learned the art of meditation.* Once we know cycling, we can ride bicycles under any conditions and in all places. But while we are learning we will have to practice on open ground and follow the rules of balance for our own convenience and for the convenience of others around us. Similarly, for the beginning meditator it is advisable to start meditation in the pose explained above, preferably in front of a form that symbolizes God for him.

Thought-Parade

With the physical body properly adjusted to begin meditation, you must next consider how to prepare your mental equipment for the contemplative flight.

The human mind functions on three levels—the conscious, the subconscious, and the unconscious. The *conscious* is the surface mind, containing thoughts we have fully realized. Unfinished

69

thoughts, undigested experiences, mutilated ideas, crushed emotions, suffocated desires—thoughts that have met with conflict—
sink into our personality and are held in suspension in the *subconscious* mind. The *unconscious* is constituted of impulses, instincts, and emotions that are unknown to us, but that come up and
express themselves under certain stress of circumstances. The
unconscious is equivalent to the causal body (*vāsanās*, in Vedantic
terminology).

Whenever the conscious mind is quiet, the subconscious has
a chance to float up. Manifestations of the subconscious on the
platform of the conscious mind are generally experienced in dreams.
In this sense, we can say that dreams are nature's exhaust pipes
through which tensions and pressures created in the mind are
released. When an individual moves away from the conscious
mind, crowded with its preoccupations, problems, and the never-
ending hosts of stimuli received from outside, and reaches into
peaceful sleep, the agitated, conscious mind becomes relatively
quiet; this is the sacred hour when nature purges the mind of its
subconscious accumulations. Thus, between sleep and waking, the
quieted conscious mind becomes the platform upon which the
mutilated ideas, unassimilated thoughts, and unseemly motives—
until now putrefying in the subconscious mind—emerge and dance
away in our dreams.

If this phenomenon is properly understood, we can directly
realize the benefit accrued from congregational prayers or ritualistic celebrations in the temple, church, mosque, or vihar. On all such
occasions we conscientiously make our conscious minds quiet,
allowing the subconscious mind to float up. After this purging, we
experience a greater lightness of heart, and the personality gets
temporarily released from its constrictions.

Such purging becomes even more effectual when the seeker
sits alone for meditation, prayer, or *japa*.[2] Often, when the seeker
reaches the prayer room and starts his prayers, vulgar, immoral
thoughts—the presence of which he had not even suspected—
come gushing forth in irresistible flow. The student who applies
himself to meditation brings about a conscious state of quiet, and at
that moment of relative peace of the conscious mind the subconscious
dirt emerges out. This ugly upheaval constitutes the disturbing
drama that often frightens and discourages newly initiated seekers.

---

[2] *Japa* is discussed in detail in Chapter 16.

In preparing yourself for meditation, it is important that you allow all such disturbing thoughts, or any other predominant thoughts already in the mind, to rise to the surface to exhaust themselves. Do not try to suppress them. However, be careful not to initiate any fresh thoughts either, for, by doing so, the mental agitations will again increase instead of decreasing. As the predominant thoughts exhaust themselves, identify with your intellect and let it stand firm as a detached witness of the thoughts rising and passing away. The intellect acts exactly as a commanding officer in an army parade when he takes the salute and watches the soldiers marching past him without himself identifying with any one of the soldiers of the parade. By this practice, all the agitations in the mind will subside, at least temporarily, making the mind available for meditation. This process is called *thought-parade*.

In the beginning this practice will not be easy. The subconscious will not always come up at your will, since some thoughts may be uncomfortable or frightening. Because of this very reason, unfinished thoughts get tucked away in the subconscious. But if you stand apart like an interested but unattached observer, they will begin to flow freely.

A little goading will help in the beginning. As you settle down for *japa*, meditation, or prayer, bring to your memory a beautiful scene, a memorable incident in your life, the most complete joy you ever experienced, an arresting landscape captured by your memory, or the face of the one whom you love the most or the one whom you hate the most. By such goading, the thought-flow can be set at large. Then stand apart to watch the procession of thoughts. Remember, once the floodgates are open, you have no chance of escaping the sweeping flow. Stand apart, or you will be carried away by the flood. If you stand apart from the lashing flow of thoughts, the flow shall, in time, end of its own accord, and the mind will be emptied of the subconscious dross. The conscious mind, released from the pressure of the subconscious, becomes lighter and achieves flight into the subtler fields of meditative joys.

These instructions, when written out and read point by point, may seem difficult and confusing; but once you start practicing, the procedure will become automatic and easy.

"Failures" in meditation bring greater gains than success in life. Sincerity and regularity are the secrets of success in meditation. Contact with a guru and constant study of the scriptures are factors that can guarantee success.

Inquire,
Then Contemplate 14

The seeker may suspect that the precise prescriptions on proper posture for meditation and other physical details are too elaborate for the purpose of religious prayer and meditation. Such feelings are natural. Prayer should be easy and straightforward. There cannot be any mechanical exercises for meditation. And yet, we have described various physical, mental, and intellectual adjustments and exercises. A contradiction seems to exist here. There are justifications that explain why the seers left such detailed instructions.

In the scheme of evolution from animal to man, various levels of subtle growth were experienced. In the beginning, the human being was in a state of mere *perception*. He perceived things around him and reacted instinctively. He had no chance to bring the play of his intellect into the field of his perceptions because his intellect had not yet evolved. In this *Age of Perception*, humankind in its childhood stage felt happy when perceptions were harmonious with the mental moods. Thunder and lightning, the roar of lions, and the staggering noise of waterfalls were disconcerting, for they brought disharmony into the mind. In fear and confusion the man of this age escaped to safety, prompted by his inherent instinct for self-preservation.

Later, man's intellectual capacities developed, and his perceptions began to be supported by his intellect. Intelligent perception is called observation. Thus, from the realms of perception the human being climbed to a higher plateau of *observation*. He started questioning his perceptions—why? how? when? where? This was the *Age of Observation.* But since man's intellect was still crude, his analysis could not go very far, and all that he gathered was only superstition, not knowledge.

In time, the intellect became more assertive and gained a sharpness that was not even suspected in the earlier stages of evolution. Thus, superstitions were thrown over, and man sauntered into the *Age of Inquiry and Investigation*, wherein his unfolded intellect logically came to apprehend the laws of nature. He initiated the Era of Science.

Man's vision of the world changed as he moved from the Age of Perception through the Age of Observation into the Age of Inquiry. From the life of perception with its instinctive joys and sorrows, he marched into the dark caves of superstitious knowledge, and finally into the fields of daring science. And at each stage, he never failed to laugh at his forefathers and their stupidities.

Today, we stand on the summit of science. We laugh at the crude past with its confusions and wrong notions. It is clear to us that the man of perception could not understand or suspect the vision of the man of observation, and that the man of observation could never have dreamed of the possibilities achieved by the man of inquiry and investigation. Historically it is true that the man of observation was not appreciated by the man of perception. The evolved one was condemned and laughed at. History also tells us how the first systematic observers of the world who initiated the age of science were persecuted by the powerful men of the age of superstition. Today, in the scientific age, the prophetic seers and philosophers, the evolved men of a future age, stand condemned by the men of inquiry and investigation. History repeats itself, and the student learns his lessons from its repeated revelations.

Thus, if today the great scientists of the world fail to realize the glory of true religion, it is not altogether inexplicable. They conquer outer space, they may occupy Mars or the Moon, but they will not understand the vision of religious masters and philosophers because these men of inner knowledge and spirituality have a more evolved intellect than the scientists.

The fourth stage of development of the human intellect is contemplation. The power of contemplation is already inherent in us, but it has not yet fully manifested itself. Just as every child has a dormant sex impulse waiting to manifest itself when biological growth is complete, so too the power of contemplation is dormant in everyone and is waiting to become manifest. All scriptures are words of wisdom given by people of contemplation to students who have cultivated in themselves this subtle evolutionary perfection.

The experience gained, knowledge acquired, and notions gathered about the riddle of life through contemplation is philosophy. Philosophy is taught by contemplative individuals to students who have developed a contemplative mind. Meditation is the process by which the seeker develops his dormant faculty of contemplation. Naturally, if the processes explained here seem rather mechanical, they are so only while you read about them. Once you come to the seat of meditation, you will realize that they are actually self-evolving processes that are at once scientific and spiritually effective. As you read, you are a person of inquiry; when you sit down for meditation, you become a person of contemplation.

And is not our world silently moving from the Age of Inquiry and Science into the *Age of Contemplation and Meditation*? Your father and grandmothers may not have even heard of these terms, while in your times contemplation and meditation have become popular, and many like you have started contemplative practice.

Train the Mind 15

In all religions we hear about the necessity for controlling the mind. The mind is thought-flow. Just as water flowing continuously in a given direction is a river, so thoughts flowing continuously from an individual to the world of objects is the mind. The character of a river is determined by the character of its waters. If the water is clean, the river is clean. If the water's flow is fast, the river is fast. Similarly, the mind is conditioned by its thoughts. The nature and behavior of thoughts in an individual at a given moment condition and define his mind. If his thoughts are good, his mind is good. If his thoughts are agitated, his mind is agitated. In fact, it is but true to say, "As the thoughts, so the mind; as the mind, so the man."

If a seeker demands a total transformation of his personality and strives to become a God-man, he must tackle his mind and bring it under his control. To tame a river is to tame the flow of the waters in it. To tame the mind, the seeker has to change the *quality*, the *quantity*, and the *direction* of its thought-flow. This program will achieve total transformation of his personality and bring about his inner resurrection.

The *quality* of thoughts in our mind depends on the type of objects that initiate or sustain our thoughts. The company of good books and noble people, dynamic aspiration and inspiring ideals—all these can change the quality of our thought-pattern. By surrender to the Lord, by unbroken remembrance of Him and His absolute virtues, by supreme love, and a divine sense of justice, the quality of thoughts in the devotee's mind is improved by association. Devotion to God (*bhakti yoga*) is the means by which the quality of thoughts is improved.

A river that is flooded and flowing at a terrific velocity cannot be easily controlled or directed. To tame the river, we have to wait until the flood subsides. Similarly, the human mind will sweep down, with its own flooded might, all our attempts at controlling or modifying its patterns. The quieted mind alone is available for remolding.

In most of us, the mind is always in a state of dangerous flooding. Thoughts thunder and roar in their sweep among objects, feelings, and ideas. This state of flood is aggravated by three main streams, which are the main sources of the river-of-thought: (a) memories of the past, (b) anxieties for the future, and (c) excitements in the present. The control of these three sources of thought-flow is the process by which the dimension, velocity, force, and sweep of the flood of the mind are controlled.

Selfless, dedicated activities undertaken as an offering at the altar of our ideal, in a spirit of surrender to the Lord, is the only method by which we can save our mind from these disastrous floods. When we follow an ideal, we can surrender at its altar our regrets of the past, our anxieties for the future, and our excitements in the present. If we work in this spirit of dedication and surrender to the Lord, the mind becomes peaceful. When such work becomes a habit, the personality of the selfless worker (karma yogi) is tamed for remolding.

If the quality of thoughts is changed by following the path of devotion (bhakti yoga), and the quantity of thoughts is controlled by pursuing the path of dedicated action (karma yoga), then the direction of thoughts is changed by the pursuit of the path of knowledge (jñāna yoga).

To lift ourselves from our identification with the body, mind, and intellect, and to end our concept of ourselves as perceivers, feelers, and thinkers, we must seek to redirect our thoughts in search of the infinite Self, which expresses Itself through these vehicles. Extrovertedness of the mind brings agitations and chaos. As thoughts gather momentum, the individual is swept in the direction of devolution, sorrow, and animalism. The quest for the source of all activities, for the presence of divinity within, constitutes changing the direction of one's thoughts. In this state of introvertedness of the mind, the thoughts become peaceful and serene.

These three processes are not mutually exclusive. Each is not separate from the other but is complementary to the other two. Quality cannot be changed without consciously or unconsciously changing the quantity and direction of the thoughts also. Unless the quality and quantity are modified, the direction of thought-flow cannot be changed. And when the quantity of thoughts is diminished, the quality and direction of thoughts are also changed.

The paths of devotion, action, and knowledge are to be practiced in synthesis, although you may take one or the other of them as your main path according to your temperament. However, each student shall find that, whatever be his main path, the other two paths cannot be totally eliminated from his program of self-evolution. Since the paths for changing the quality, quantity, and direction of thoughts are so intrinsically interrelated, the accomplishment of one is at once the fulfillment of the other two. Hence the importance of *japa*, in which all these three come into full play at once.

Japa Yoga

16

Japa yoga is a method of mental training by which the ever-dancing rays of the mind are compelled to behave in order and rhythm through the continuous chanting of a chosen mantra, or name of God. If *japa* is practiced effectively, it can bring about sustained single-pointedness. In fact, properly done, *japa* can more effectively bring about a sustained single-pointedness than hasty methods of meditation. A *japa*-conditioned mind can go to unimaginable heights in a very short period of meditation.

Japa trains the mind to fix itself to a single line of thinking. We cannot pronounce a word without a corresponding thought-form rising up in us; nor can we have a thought-form without its corresponding name. Repeat the word *pen*, and you will see a pen in your mind's eye. This close connection between name and form constitutes the underlying principle in the technique of *japa yoga.*

Again, love is not generated where sufficient thought has not been bestowed. You love your own child more than your uncle's sister-in-law's nephew. You may admire him, yet not love him, simply because you have not spent sufficient thought on that child. *Japa* performed with intensity in the meditation seat and the mental repetition of God's name throughout the waking hours are sure ways of developing devotion. It is always the repetition of thinking that brings about the fastness in our attachments. The less we think about a thing, the less we become attached to it. The opposite is equally true: the more we think about a thing, the more we get attached to it.

In meditation one is wingless if one has not acquired the power of concentration and the knowledge of how to fix one's mind at will on a single thought for a length of time. Meditation is keeping the mind hitched to one line of thinking, to the complete exclusion of all dissimilar thought-currents. To succeed in meditation one must learn to stop at will all thought-currents but the chosen focus of one's meditation. *Japa* can help develop this mental capacity.

Japa yoga is a very effective mental discipline for spiritual progress. In recent history there is the instance of the esteemed teacher of Shivaji, Samartha Ramdas, who perfected himself through the *japa yoga* of the "*Śrī Rāma*" mantra: "*Om Śrī Rāma, Jaya Rāma, Jaya, Jaya Rāma.*" Lord Krishna Himself says in the *Bhagavad Gītā*, "I am, among the yogas, *japa yoga.*"

Procedure

Designate a special room or place for your spiritual practice. Install a picture of the Lord at such a height from the floor that when you sit in front of it, the Lord's feet will be level with your eyes. Spread a small rug in front of the picture, and have ready a *mālā* (rosary) of 108 beads.[1] Start your *japa* behind closed doors, sitting in any comfortable legs-folded position.

Look at the Lord's face, body, legs, feet. Now slowly raise your gaze up from the feet, legs, and body to the face of the Lord. Close your eyes. Feel His presence within and try to visualize the Lord exactly as He appears in the picture. This visualization of the Lord should occur within your "love heart," which is on the right side of your physical heart. This is the spiritual heart-center in you. If you meditate on it, your success is doubly assured.

Repeat your chosen mantra a few times, slowly, steadily, and with love. This will invoke the feeling of devotion in you to do *japa* most effectively. Take the *mālā* and search for the off-bead, the *meru*. Bring the tips of your ring finger and thumb together, and let the *mālā* hang at this junction; now let the *mālā*-holding palm rest on your knee. Repeat your mantra fervently, and at each repetition turn one bead with your middle finger and thumb, toward yourself, always allowing the index finger to stand apart. The index finger is considered an "outcast." This finger is generally used when pointing out another, in accusing another, when threatening, and so on. Essentially, the index finger is used to express duality and the otherness of things and beings.

---

[1] The Hindu *mālā* generally consists of 108 beads strung together on a single cord with a small space between the individual beads. The 108 beads correspond to the 108 extant Upanishads of the Vedas.

ı existence – not destroyed or lost

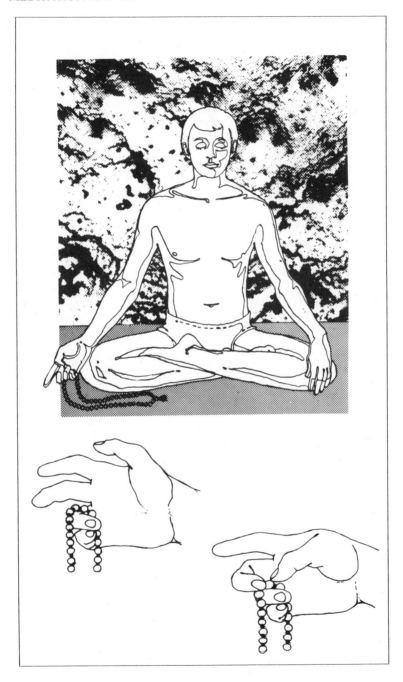

When you have repeated your chosen mantra 108 times, with the turning of the 108 beads of the *mala* , you will reach back to the *meru* bead. You have now completed one *mala*. Don't cross the *meru*. Turn the *mala* in such a way that the 109th mantra is counted on the bead with which the 107th mantra was registered. Then finish your second *mala* of *japa*.

Mantras

A mantra is a word-symbol or symbols expressing, as nearly as possible, a particular view of God and the universe. When a person first begins to learn writing, she draws big scrawls before she can successfully try a smaller hand. So too a person must acquire the power of concentrating her thoughts by fixing her mind first on divine forms; then, after fair success therein, by fixing it on the formless Divine. There is nothing secret about these mantras. All of them are in the scriptures, but when a mantra is given to a disciple by an illumined teacher, it becomes a living seed. The teacher, by his spiritual power, gives life to the word, and at the same time awakens the spiritual powers latent in the disciple. That is the secret of the teacher's initiation. A sampling of mantras is given below. Any one of them can be taken up according to one's taste, faith, and devotion:

Vedantic Mantras

Tat Tvamasi: That thou art.
Aham Brahmasmi: I am *Brahman*.
Ayam Atma Brahma: This Self is *Brahman*.
Śivoham, Śivoham: I am Shiva, auspiciousness.
Tadeva Satyam Tat Brahma: That alone is the Truth,
   That is *Brahman*.
Anandoham, Anandoham: I am *ananda*, I am bliss.
Hamsah Soham, Soham Hamsah: I am He, He am I;
   He am I, I am He.

Puranic Mantras:

Om Namo Narayanaya
Om Śri Rama, Jaya Rama, Jaya, Jaya Rama
Om Namah Śivaya
Om Śri Sanmukhaya Namaha
Om Śri Ramacandraya Namaha
Om Śri Laksmyai Namaha

Cautions

While doing *japa*, remember that even though the posture, the bead-rolling, the chosen deity, and such other details are external, *japa* in itself is not physical but mental, and is to be raised to a still higher level. Neither a mere rolling of the beads nor a nonstop muttering of the mantra constitutes *japa yoga*. *Japa* should be an all-out intense and sincere effort to bring forth from one's mind and intellect all the possible higher faculties—like love, discrimination, sensitivity, will, logic, reason, sympathy, faith—and pour them all into concentrating on the mental chanting of the sacred mantra.

This seemingly simple yoga should not be overpracticed. Start with one *mālā* of *japa* a day. Slowly raise the number of *mālās*. You might start by increasing the number of *mālās* at first on convenient holidays only, and when you are convinced of your mental capacity to sustain your attention for the required period of time, take to long sittings at *japa*. Eventually you may be able to do twenty *mālās* twice a day, once in the morning and once in the evening.

Japa generally enchants the unwary practitioner into unproductive thought-wanderings. If the student is not diligent and does not arrest his thoughts, it is possible that his *japa* will cause frustration and stupor. A common difficulty is an irresistible need to sleep while doing *japa* and a tendency to express bad temper soon after the *japa* session. The seeker should not feel discouraged, but should learn to fight these tendencies patiently.

The need to sleep is strong because a mind in *japa* is a mind at rest. Bad temper comes about because of two reasons—suppression of tendencies and fatigue. The former starts with the *japist's* own annoyance at seeing his mind wander here and there during his *japa*. The latter is caused by exhaustion, for to hold the mind in balance on a given line of thought, particularly for the beginner, is a great strain, and therefore the mind gets fatigued.

A new driver at the wheel does not know how to relax, and therefore he unnecessarily exhausts himself before he has driven around the first corner of his own street; a new swimmer will feel fatigued after a few yards; a new housewife gets tired from looking after her firstborn. Later on that very same woman easily manages her half-a-dozen offspring, yet finds for herself plenty of spare time and mental ease.

One must learn the art of economizing energy. Every type of

work requires its own measure of stamina that must be drawn from the individual personality. This requirement holds equally true in all spiritual activities. One's subtle judgment in evaluating works of art is not a skill that can be taught, but it is a capacity that one discovers for oneself as one practices. The same rule applies in the art of spiritual practice. The practitioner himself will have to discover the rhythm and harmony of successful spiritual practice, which will come as a result of continuous practice in the right direction.

Regularity and sincerity are the secrets of success in any spiritual endeavor, including *japa yoga*. Guard the mind against all excesses and make it immune to selfishness and passion. Watch how imperceptibly the mind ties itself down to things, beings, happenings, and circumstances by its own unintelligent attachments. Even when all these warnings are faithfully followed, we may still encounter the subtle danger that our *japa* activity will be muddled with our incorrigible thirst for fruits.

The profit motive is the strongest urge in man in all his activities. *Japa*, polluted by this profit motive, will not end in spiritual effulgence. Approach your *japa* in surrender. Gather the purest and the best within you and offer that to your *japa* as a devoted oblation. The potential strength of blessing that lies dormant in *japa* will then be invoked. The effectiveness of *japa* largely depends on your spirit of surrender. This idea of surrender should not be merely an emotional explosion, but should be instead an act of understanding, deliberate and conscious. Once we understand the principle behind surrender, we discover the bridge that connects *bhakti* to *jñāna*.

Let us, for example, take a typical mantra and try to discover the attitude of surrender implied in it: *Om Namo Nārāyanāya*—"My prostrations unto Narayana."[2]

Prostration is not merely a physical act, but is a conscious effort of discovering the Highest and seeking our identity with It. To tune ourselves with the better or the nobler, and thereby gather unto ourselves the qualities and greatness of the Higher, is true prostration. In order to prostrate, two factors must be present: the lesser who prostrates and the Higher at whose feet the prostrations

---

[2] Narayana is a name of Vishnu, God in the aspect of Preserver.

are offered. Within each one of us there is the matter-conditioned ego and the unconditioned eternal Self. The *japist* tries to end his false ego at the altar of himself—the supremely divine Self, Sri Narayana. Thus, in his practice of *japa*, the student strives to surrender his personality totally to Narayana, who is his concept of Reality.

A mantra is a formula that explains not only what is the enduring Truth in life, but also the technique by which we can reach it. *Om*[3] is the symbol of the Infinite, which is finally attained through surrender of all our false identifications with the matter envelopments at the feet of Narayana. When the concept of an individual personality is removed from us, we come to experience the existence of Narayana in ourselves, which, being the same everywhere and at all times, is itself the experience of *Om*, *Brahman*, the supreme Reality.

---

[3] *Om* is the first word of the mantra "*Om Namo Nārāyaṇāya.*"

The Sacred Mantra Om

17

Mantras are given out by the people of wisdom who have realized the deep significance of the syllable. Every mantra has a presiding deity. The belief is that when one chants a mantra, he or she should keep in mind the form of that deity. Then, just as someone who responds upon being called by his name, the deity of the mantra is invoked by the chanting. It is also the belief that only after chanting a mantra for a hundred thousand times can we hope to see any benign influence of the *japa* practice.

Three types of mantras are described: those that invoke the low powers of nature (*tāmasic*); those that excite and manifest might and power (*rājasic*); and those that lead to spiritual experience (*sāttvic*).

All mantras fall under two further classifications: (a) those that are simply to be chanted, with no need to understand their meaning; and (b) those that are of the nature of an invocation and require the devotee to know their meaning, without which he or she will be unable to bring the mind to play upon the divine theme. The Vedic mantras appear both in poetry and in prose.

Of all the mantras the most powerful and significant one is the single-syllable incantation called the *Pranava*—the *Om*.

From Vedic times until the present day, spiritual aspirants have used *Om* chanting as an aid to meditation. *Om* is accepted as being both one with *Brahman* and also as the medium that connects the human being to God. The entire history of the syllable is in the revelations of the Vedas and in the declarations of the Upanishads. A verse in the Vedas says, "In the beginning was Prajapati, the *Brahman*, with Whom was the Word. And the Word was verily the supreme *Brahman*." This Sphota has its symbol in the syllable *Om*.[1]

---

[1] *Sphota* literally means "the idea or sound that makes the mind open like a blossom" and is comparable to Logos, the sound-essence that is the

Thus, in the *Maitrāvana Upaniṣad*, after it has been said that there is one *Brahman* without words, and a second, a word-*Brahman*, we are told that the word is the syllable *Om*. The sound of *Om* is also called *Praṇava*, meaning that it is something that pervades life, or runs through one's *prāṇa*, or breath.

The central theme of the *Māṇḍūkya Upaniṣad* is the syllable *Om*, through which the mystery of *Brahman* is gathered to a point. The text of this Upanishad treats *Om* in terms of the Upanishadic doctrine of the three states of waking, dream, and deep sleep, but then passes on to the fourth state, thus transporting us beyond the typical Upanishadic sphere into that of the later classical Advaita Vedanta (Nondualistic Vedanta). Speaking of *Om*, the *Taittirīya Upaniṣad* says, "Thou art the sheath of *Brahman*"; that is, *Om* is the container for the Supreme, and therefore invoking *Om* is invoking the Supreme.

Om has three aspects. The first is the mere sound, the mantra as pronounced by the mouth; the second is the meaning of the syllable, which one must realize through feeling; and the third is the application of *Om* to one's character, in one's actions and life.

Om represents the Self, which is the supreme, nondual Reality. The Self is known in four states, namely, the waking state, the dream state, the deep-sleep state, and the fourth state called the *turīya*. All these states are represented in the three sounds of *Om* (*A, U, M*)[2] and the silence that follows and surrounds the syllable. The sound *A* represents the waking state; the sound *U* represents the dream state; and the sound *M* represents the deep-sleep state.

The waking state is superimposed on the *A* sound because it is the first of the three states of consciousness, and the sound *A* is the very first letter in the alphabet—in any language. The dream is but a view within the mind of the impressions reflected on the surface of the mental lake during the waking state. The dream state occurs between the waking and the deep-sleep states, and is second among the three states of consciousness. And so, since *U* is next to

---

controlling principle of the universe. A similar idea is repeated in the Fourth Gospel of the New Testament: "In the beginning was the Word, and the Word was with God, and the Word was God" (John 1:1).

[2] In Sanskrit the vowel *o* is a diphthong, composed of *a* and *u*. Thus, *Om* can also be written *Aum*.

A in the order of sounds in *Om*, and also between *A* and *M*, it is used to represent the dream state. The deep-sleep state is superimposed on the *M* sound of *Om*. The comparison between the last sound of *Om* and deep sleep is based on the fact that it is the closing sound of the syllable, just as deep sleep is the final stage of the mind at rest. A short, pregnant silence is inevitable between two successive utterings of *Om*. On this silence is superimposed the idea of the fourth state, known as *turīya*. This is the state of perfect bliss when the individual self recognizes its identity with the Supreme.

In *Om* the sounds *A*, *U*, and *M* are called *mātrās*, or forms. The silence that follows the *Om* chant and the common principle that pervades it is called the *Amātra-Om*, that which signifies the thing-in-itself, pervading the threefold phenomenon of waking, dream, and deep sleep. Memory is impossible unless the rememberer and the experiencer are one and the same individual. In all three planes, there must necessarily be a single common factor that is the witness of all the happenings in the three planes. There must be some entity within ourselves who is present in the waking world, who moves and illumines the dream, and who is a distant observer in the deep-sleep world—but who is not conditioned by any of these three realms. This entity, conceived as the fourth state (*turīya*), is the real, the changeless, the intelligent principle.

The syllable *Om* symbolizes two spheres: (a) the phenomenal, visible sphere wherein the manifestations of time and space appear and perish, and (b) the transcendent, timeless sphere of imperishable being, which is beyond the phenomenal sphere yet one with it. Thus, *A*, the waking state, *U*, the dream state, *M*, the deep-sleep state, and the silence, *turīya*—all the four together, as one syllable, comprise the totality of the manifestation of *Ātman-Brahman*. Just as the sound *M* manifests itself, grows, becomes transformed in its vocal quality, and finally subsides into the silence that follows, so too the three states of being ultimately merge into the homogeneous silence of the *turīya*. The three states are transformations of the one experience; together, they constitute the totality of the modes of the one experience, whether regarded from the microcosmic or macrocosmic point of view. The *A* and *U* are as essential to the sound as *M*, as is the silence against which the sounds appear. Moreover, it would be incorrect to say that *Om* does not exist while the silence reigns, for it is still present even in the silence. The actual manifestation of the syllable, on the other hand, is fleeting and

evanescent, whereas the silence abides. The silence, indeed, is
present even during the pronunciation of *A-U-M*; by analogy, it is
present as transcendent and immanent during the creation, manifestation, and dissolution of the universe.

Often it is asked why this particular word *Om* was chosen as
the representative of the "thought" out of which the universe
manifested itself. The answer may be given in Swami Vivekananda's
words:

> ... this *Om* is the only possible symbol which covers the
> whole ground, and there is none other like it. The
> Sphota is the material of all words, yet it is not any
> definite word in its fully formed state. That is to say, if
> all the particularities which distinguish one word from
> another be removed, then what remains will be the
> Sphota; therefore, this Sphota is called the *Nāda-Brahma*,
> the *Sound-Brahman*.
>
> Now, as every word-symbol, intended to express the
> inexpressible Sphota, will so particularize it that it will
> no longer be the Sphota, that symbol which particular-
> izes it the least and at the same time most approximately
> expresses its nature will be the truest symbol thereof;
> and this is the *Om*, and the *Om* only; because these three
> letters (*A-U-M*), pronounced in combination as *Om*, may
> well be the generalized symbol of all possible sounds.
> The letter *A* is the least differentiated of all sounds ....
> Again, all articulate sounds are produced in the space
> within the mouth beginning with the root of the tongue
> and ending in the lips—the throat sound is *A*, and *M* is
> the last lip sound, and the *U* exactly represents the
> rolling forward of the impulse which begins at the root
> of the tongue till it ends in the lips. If properly pro-
> nounced, this *Om* will represent the whole phenomenon
> of sound production, and no other word can do this; and
> this, therefore, is the fittest symbol of the Sphota, which
> is the real meaning of the *Om*. And as the symbol can
> never be separated from the thing signified, the *Om* and
> the Sphota are one. And as the Sphota, being the finer
> side of the manifest universe, is nearer to God, and is

indeed the first manifestation of divine wisdom, this *Om* is truly symbolic of God.[3]

Every mantra includes the *Praṇava, Om.* Without *Om* no sacred chant has power. Just as a living body has no vitality when the life-giving breath has ceased, so too a mantra has no life in it without *Om.*

Om represents both the manifest and the unmanifest, which together constitute the entire gross and subtle worlds. It also represents that which lies beyond both the manifest and the unmanifest—the *Brahman,* which is the changeless substratum for the changing objects of the world of experiences. All possibilities of experience in life have been terraced by the rishis into fourteen worlds, or *lokas:*[4] seven higher worlds and seven lower worlds. There are three worlds in which a limited ego comes to play its game of reincarnation and repeated deaths: Bhur-Loka, the physical earth; Bhuvar-Loka, the world next to the physical and closely connected with it, but constituted of finer matter; and Svar-Loka, the heavenly world. Beyond these are the four worlds wherein the ego moves about and enjoys its higher evolutionary life. These are called the Mahar-Loka, Jana-Loka, Tapo-Loka, and Satya-Loka.

Below these seven worlds, there is yet another set of seven worlds called the *talas.* They are named Pa-Tala, Maha-Tala, Rasa-Tala, Tala-Tala, Su-Tala, Vi-Tala, and A-Tala.

Of these fourteen worlds, Bhur-Bhuvar-Svar, denoting the "three worlds," are called the *Vyāhṛtis.* In the *Gāyatrī Mantra,* a major Vedic mantra discussed in detail in Chapter 18, when these *Vyāhṛtis* are chanted, the meditator can visualize the three worlds arising from, existing in, and disappearing into *Om.* He can subjectively identify them with the waking, dream, and deep-sleep conditions of consciousness, transcending which extends the realm of the Infinite. All of them are represented in the symbol *Om.* In this sense, the *Vyāhṛtis* in the *Gāyatrī Mantra* represent in one sweep the entire world of the subjective and objective experiences of humankind.

---

[3] From "The Mantra: Om: Word and Wisdom," in "Bhakti-Yoga," *The Complete Works of Swami Vivekananda,* Vol. III, pp. 57-58. Calcutta, India: Advaita Ashrama, 1955.

[4] The word *loka* in Sanskrit is generally translated as "world," but in its etymological meaning it only signifies "a field of experience."

The Gāyatrī
Mantra

18

Om Bhūr Bhuvas Suvaḥ[1]
Om Tat Savitur vareṇyam
Bhargo Devasya dhimahi
Dhiyo yo naḥ pracodayāt

The above is how the *Gāyatrī Mantra* is traditionally chanted; but the mantra proper contains only three lines, without the *Vyāhṛtis* (the names of the three worlds—Bhur, Bhuvar, Svar), and omits the initial *Om* in the line *"Tat Savitur vareṇyam."* The mantra proper may be translated as follows:

> *We meditate upon the auspicious, godly light of the Lord Sun; may that heavenly light illumine the thought-flow in our intellect.*

The Hindu concept that the *Gāyatrī Mantra* was first declared by the Creator Himself at the very beginning of creation may be considered an overexaggeration—an unavoidable feature in many portions of Vedic literature. But it is a fact that even Western scholars who are accepted historical authorities have declared the *Gāyatrī Mantra* as one of the oldest available hymns. It is not only believed, but also has been actually observed, that by the repetition of this mantra, with the right understanding of its sacred meaning, the ordinary negative tendencies in the human mind can be to a large extent erased.

This mantra is never chanted for the purpose of material or

---

[1] *Bhuvas* is the same word as *Bhuvar*, and *Suvaḥ* is the same word as *Svar*, the variations resulting from the requirements of Sanskrit grammar.

other gains. It is an invocation that concludes with an appeal to the
pure Consciousness to unveil Itself and come to manifest as pure
wisdom in our life.

The *Gāyatrī* is an invocation dedicated to the Lord Sun,
couched in the Vedic meter called *Gāyatrī*; therefore, this sacred
mantra has come to be known as the *Gāyatrī Mantra.* It is found
recorded in the *Ṛg Veda*, the most ancient of the four Vedas. The
Gāyatrī meter is generally constituted of three lines of eight syllables each. The three lines of the *Gāyatrī Mantra* are:

> *Tat Savitur vareṇyam*
> *Bhargo Devasya dhimahi*
> *Dhiyo yo naḥ pracodayāt*

You will find in the above that the first line has only seven
syllables. This is explained generally in two ways: (a) the syllable
nyam is constituted of *ni* plus *am*, thus producing the required eight
syllables in the line, and (b) the line is to be read along with the
Praṇava, Om, which would supply the missing syllable. The former
is the explanation of Sri Shankaracharya, the great Vedantic master,
in his brilliant commentary on the *Bṛhadāraṇyaka Upaniṣad.*

This mantra is dedicated to the Lord Savitr.[2] That Savitr represents Lord Sun is the accepted version, although some scholars
protest against this interpretation. The sun gives all illumination to
the world, and any prayer for light should certainly be addressed
to the source of all light in the material world, the sun. In the *Bhagavad
Gītā* Lord Krishna says, "The light that pervades the sun and the
moon is all My light." Thus, Savitr, the Lord of *Gāyatrī*, is nothing
other than the Light of Consciousness, the Infinite, the Absolute:
"We meditate upon the auspicious, godly light of the Lord Sun.
May that heavenly light illumine the thought-flow in our intellect."

In our own inner life, the sun represents the illuminator of all
experiences, the *Ātman*. This pure Consciousness in us, around
which the matter envelopments function—just as the entire solar
system revolves around the sun—is being invoked to shine more
fully in our intellect. If the sun were not there, physical life on earth
would be impossible. Without *Ātman*, the matter envelopments
would become inert. In chanting the *Gāyatrī Mantra*, the devotee is

---

[2] *Savitr* is the same word as *Savitur.*

MEDITATION AND LIFE

actually praying for spiritual unfoldment: "May my intellect be
steady without agitations; may it be clean without the dirt of
passions. May the light of Consciousness come to shine forth its
radiance through my intellect. Thus, may my perception of the
world be clear, my discrimination subtle, my judgments correct
and quick, my comprehension of situations precise and wise."

The usual prescribed daily worship of a Hindu includes
repetition of this *Gāyatrī Mantra*. From ancient days, the daily prayer
has been considered a purifactory act, a method of reintegrating
one's mind, which has run wild during the day and become
drowned completely in total inertia during the night.

In *Manusmṛti*[3] we read: "In the early dawn by doing this *japa*,
while standing, one ends all sins committed during the night; and
by doing this *japa* in the evening while sitting, one ends one's sins
committed during the day." Sin here means the agitation created
in the mind by our own negative actions, and the tendency to repeat
these actions as a result of impressions (*vāsanās*) left in our mind.

Each day has two *sandhyās*, a *sandhyā* being the blending point
of day and night. In the ancient literature we fail to find any
importance given to midday worship. According to Vedic literature, the rishis seem to insist only upon morning and evening
prayers. In the early morning when the east blushes in light and in
the evening when the day's golden light fades into darkness, we
have the two *sandhyās*. Generally, the morning prayers are done
most profitably between 4:30 and 5 o'clock, and in the evening the
interval between 6 and 7 o'clock is the sacred hour for prayers. In
the *Manusmṛti*[4] we find very interesting and clear directions on
these prayers and worship:

> After getting up from bed, after answering the calls of
> nature, purifying yourself completely, disallowing the
> mind to wander hither and thither, sincerely perform the
> morning *japa* standing on your feet and repeating the
> mantra very, very slowly.

---

[3] *Manusmṛti* 102. *Manusmṛti* is an ancient textbook on codes of conduct
written by the lawgiver Manu. Manu's code is the foundation for all Hindu
religious and social conduct.

[4] *Manusmṛti* 101.

Elsewhere in the *Manusmṛti,* we also read:

> In the morning worship, till the sun rises above the
> horizon, do the *japa* standing; and in the evening
> worship, until the stars emerge, do your *japa* sitting
> down.

The Vedas advise us to sing the *Gāyatrī Mantra* both at dawn
and at dusk while standing in water facing the sun. In the morning
the face should be turned eastward, and in the evening, westward.
The Vedas further advise that while chanting the mantra one
should hold water in one's folded palm, and at the end of each
mantra, offer that water to the Lord. As this water in the folded
palm is offered, the devotee says: "This sun is *Brahman.*" Then the
devotee turns a full turn around himself by the right, symbolizing
his reverential and devoted perambulation around the Lord Sun—
the *Brahman,* which is the Self within himself.

The *Gāyatrī* is generally chanted at each *sandhyā* a minimum
of ten times. However, according to one's faith, convenience, and
devotion, one can chant it any number of times; but this mantra is
never chanted at night after sunset.

The *Taittirīya Āraṇyaka*[5] explains in story form the reason for
the daily chanting of the *Gāyatrī* and the offering poured toward the
sun. On an island called Arunam lived a tribe of devils called
Mandehas. Every morning these devils conquered all space and
almost reached the sun, threatening to destroy him. But the water
thrown by the *Gāyatrī japists* was lightning-strong, striking the devils
and forcing them to retreat to their islands.

The story is symbolic of events in one's mind. Mind (*manas*)
and body (*deha*)[6] are the sources of our activities. With their likes,
dislikes, emotions, appetites, passions, and cravings, they bring out
our passionate animal instincts, which try to conquer and destroy
the spiritual essence—*Brahman,* or the sun—in us. The essential
brilliance of the human intellect is clouded by these passions. The
Gāyatrī Japa, with the force of lightning, descends upon them and
dissipates them.

---

[5] The *Āraṇyaka* is that portion of the Vedas which connects the purely
ritualistic section with the essentially philosophic portion, the Upanishads.
[6] Recall that the tribal name of the devils was *Mandeha.*

In India, a Hindu boy is initiated into the *Gāyatrī Mantra* very early in his life. The initiation takes place at a ritual called the *upanayana* ceremony, presided over by the head of the family and the family priest.[7] After this initiation, the boy is considered twice-born:

> The father and mother have given birth to him from mutual desire, so that he is born from the womb; let this be known as his physical birth.
>   But that birth which is given, according to the ordinance, through the Savitri by a preceptor who has mastered the Vedas, that is the true birth, the unaging and immortal.[8]

In ancient days women used to chant the *Gāyatrī* as freely as men, according to Manu. All women had participated in the *upanayana* ceremony. They used to learn the Vedas, teach the Vedas, and chant the *Gāyatrī Mantra*. In fact, women have found spiritual unfoldment through *japa yoga* more readily than men, because women have, at least in the past, not been subjected to as many of the nerve-shattering contacts of the competitive work-a-day world as men. The Hindu sacred books repeatedly declare that if the effects of spiritual practice performed by men are their own, then the spiritual benefits acquired by women are also shared by their husbands, children, and the entire society—because women mold the character of their children, and so control the quality of the society itself.

The *Gāyatrī Mantra* has a fourth and secret line mentioned in the *Chāndoggya* and *Bṛhadāraṇyaka Upaniṣads* and in the *Brahma Sūtras*. This line has been preserved as sacred and secret,[9] and is only told to fulltime seekers or to dedicated *sannyāsīs* (renunciates). The line is not so much for chanting as for experiencing the highest moments of intense meditation in *samādhi*.

---

[7] The word *upanayana* means "bringing nearer." During the ceremony, besides being initiated into the *Gāyatrī Mantra*, the boy takes vows to observe purity, truthfulness, and self-restraint. Thereafter, he can be a full participant in the Hindu faith and may perform ritualistic worship.

[8] *Manusmṛti* 147-148.

[9] "Secret" here means only that it is profound and highly subtle.

Silence the Mind

19

From our previous discussions we know that the mystics of India inquired into the nature and workings of the world of the subject, as contrasted with the world of objects, the field of the physical scientists. This choice of the rishis was not accidental. They had examined the external world exhaustively, but came to discover that the secret of the world of objects lay in the heart-world of the subject. While they were searching for Truth in the world of objects, they analyzed not only the inert world of mere objects and natural happenings, as would the modern experts of physics, chemistry, or biology, but they also examined and tried to understand the world of objects as it relates to the vital, intelligent being called man. The rishis believed that the world is but an assortment of things, which has a message and a meaning only when it comes in contact with man.

The Source of Actions

Thus, the research of the rishis naturally continued with human activity in the field of objects. Close observation revealed that no two people act the same way in the same field of exertion. This variety in human action was the first challenge the rishis examined.

Their examinations revealed that a person's actions are directly dependent upon his thoughts. The nature and quality of his actions are clear amplifications of the nature of his thoughts. They thus concluded that external actions are the gross manifestations of an individual's thoughts. When he is deprived of his thoughts, he does not perform actions. While in deep sleep, a criminal cannot be accused of committing a crime, nor can a sage be praised for performing social service.

The diligent rishis continued their analysis with an inquiry into the source of human thought. They came to the discovery that thoughts are directly controlled by our desires. Desires are the volcano from which the thought-lava erupts and flows into the field of activities. The quality and texture of our desires determine the nature of our thoughts; and our thoughts are transcribed and echoed in our actions.

The rishis then delved deeper into the human personality, searching for the source of all desires. They found that desires spring up like weeds in the soil of ignorance (*avidyā*).[1] While in reality we are the Self, pure Consciousness, we have forgotten our real nature. This self-forgetfulness is termed *ignorance* in Vedanta. Ignorance of our true nature has generated in us the concept of a mind, an intellect, a body, and a world outside. Identifying with the body, mind, and intellect, we create within ourselves a delusive identity, the limited ego.

However, no matter how strong our delusion, deep within us we have an awareness of the blissful nature of the Self. The attempt to regain this Selfhood is irresistible in all of us, and in the deluded ones this attempt is expressed in trying to acquire, hoard, spend, gain, strive, win, and so on. But the finite can never gain the Infinite through the acquisition of the finite world. That simple fact explains the sorrows of life, which dissipate only when ignorance is rooted out, revealing, in a flash, the Knowledge of the Absolute. We have then rediscovered the Self.

While we are still in ignorance, we have our various desires, which generate thought-currents, which in turn express in the outer world as actions. And actions in their reactions either thicken or remove our ignorance about our own real nature: selfish, desire-prompted actions thicken ignorance; and selfless, desireless actions lift ignorance.

Ignorance, desires, thoughts, and actions are in reality different names for one and the same factor, which manifests differently at different levels or fields of activity. *Ignorance* at the portals of the spirit becomes *desires* in the intellect, becomes *thoughts* when it plays in the mental region, and becomes *actions* when it manifests itself in the outer world of sense objects. Controlling any of these three manifestations means controlling them all, as the three are but

---

[1] Nonapprehension of Reality gives birth to many a misapprehension of the same. This "trick" of the human mind of generating nonapprehension and misapprehension is called *avidyā*.

expressions of the one primary condition—ignorance (*avidyā*, nescience).

This is the logic behind all the rules of ethics and morality, and all the prescriptions for spiritual practices in the world's religions. By controlling action, which is the grossest representation of ignorance, we purify and control our thought-currents. When our thoughts are purified, our desires are also purified. The purer the desires, the lesser the thickness of ignorance. And where ignorance has receded, Knowledge shines forth. Thus, the very process of purification of action is at once the divine process by which Knowledge is revealed.

The serious student of meditation is therefore initiated into the practice through training that insists upon a pure, ethical life. *Brahmacarya*, or abstinence from any sense indulgence in thought, word, or deed, is a necessary practice. *Brahmacarya* should not be understood as merely a measured control of sexual life. It includes all-around self-control. Any excessive indulgence through any of the sense organs—be it excessive eating, loose talking, or listening to scandal—would mean breaking the rules of *brahmacarya*. Thus prepared through right living, the sincere student of meditation goes through the preliminaries in the meditation seat, carefully adjusting his physical body in an effort to promote controlled thought-flow in meditation.

Know the Enemy

The scriptures give us a thorough definition of meditation. They define it as a process by which the meditator engages his entire mind in contemplation upon the Divine—by maintaining a steady flow of similar thought-currents to the exclusion of all dissimilar thought-intrusions, so that he can ultimately minimize his thoughts to the barest minimum, perhaps a single idea or thought.

Earlier we described the construction and workings of the subtle body, and the different names given to it according to its functions; they were the mind, intellect, *citta*, and ego. We also learned that since they are all one and the same, controlling one is controlling all. Meditation is the process by which the intellect gains dominance over the mind, and a mind so controlled becomes still. The strategy of meditation is to circumvent the pranks of the mind and thus ultimately to crush it out of existence. Naturally we can feel more confident in meditation when we fully understand the nature of the mind and its functions. To know the enemy is to forestall him.

Although only a few of us complain about the wandering mind, almost all of us are conscious of its existence. Yet rarely does a person know precisely what the mind is. Unless we know what the mind is, it is difficult for us to control it. This ignorance is the main cause for all failures of striving meditators, in spite of their diligence.

When we think about what the mind is, we always associate it with thoughts. However, we cannot say that the mind is thought. If that were true, we would have to say that we have many different minds, since few thoughts remain for more than a flashing moment. Yet certainly a very close relationship exists between thoughts and the mind. The condition and the nature of the mind depend upon the quality and texture of its thoughts. One who entertains criminal thoughts has a criminal mind, whereas saintly thoughts produce a saintly mind.

The chain of ideas is irresistible: the mind is not where thoughts are not. However, thought is not the mind. The mind is a delusory thing that seems to have potency and power when thoughts are *flowing*. When thoughts parade one after another in a continuous and unbroken stream, we have the delusory idea that a phantom power known as the mind exists.

This preliminary knowledge about the nature of the mind can help us understand how the mind can be controlled and eliminated. When our thoughts are arrested in their flow, we cannot be said to have a mind. A river is not merely water, but quantities of water flowing in a continuous, unbroken stream. If these waters are diverted, leaving only a few gallons in scattered pools in the bed of the river, we no longer can consider it a river. Similarly, when our agitated nonstop thought-currents are controlled and are made to flow steadily on a single line of thought, we have reduced the river of thought to the barest minimum. If this flow is still further reduced through intensified concentration, we shall come to a stage where the mind is said to be annihilated. The experience that remains transcends both mind and intellect. Not only in Vedanta, but in all methods of Self-realization, the culmination of all spiritual practices is this same mental annihilation. The annihilation of the mind is not to be thought of as a suicidal elimination; it is instead the sublimation of our mental and intellectual sheaths.

By physically relaxing your body, by adjusting it into a firm, neutral equilibrium, and by carefully bringing your breathing to a harmonious rhythm, you can, to a large extent, withdraw your attention from your outermost sheaths. Thereafter, your attempt in meditation will be to transcend consciously the subtle body also. This feat is at the core of the technique of meditation.

Transcend the Subtle Body

At this point you are advised to chant a mantra or to sing the glories of God, loud enough for yourself to hear. The chanting is done while sitting in front of a symbol that represents your personal concept of divinity. It might be an image of the Buddha, the Christian cross, the Koran, the symbol *Om*, or any other symbol that represents God to you. The form is your personal choice. But a symbol is unavoidable, since the human mind cannot easily conceive of an idea without a visual representation. However, accepting the symbol as the goal is a mistake. The symbol is meant only as a means for holding your mind to a single line of thought. Once you can do this, you need not depend on its use to aid the meditation process.

If *Om* is your chosen symbol, as you begin your meditation, fix your eyes on the *Om*-symbol and chant *Om* audibly and vibrantly from deep within. After chanting some five or ten times, close your eyes, but not so tightly that you become conscious of it. Let the eyelids fall shut as they would in preparing for sleep, resting gently on the eyeballs. If you have followed the instructions accurately, at this point you should be ready to concentrate. Your body is not intruding, nor is your breathing. Thus, two of the factors that normally give your mind the chance to wander have been efficiently blocked. The sense organs that now still need to be controlled are the eyes, the ears, and the tongue. However, they have been brought to work in one and the same field through audible chanting or prayer: the mouth chanted, the ears heard the chanting, and the eyes rested on your symbol of the Lord. Thus, by using most of your sense organs, you have sent into your mind a set of impulses registering practically the same sensation simultaneously.

After chanting audibly, begin mental chanting, with lips closed. You will notice at the beginning that your tongue and throat seem to strive to pronounce the words of the chant. Mentally try to watch your tongue, and make it lie relaxed on the floor of your mouth. When you have stopped the movements of the tongue, you will experience the chanting still rising in your throat. Stop this movement also. Then you will notice that it is only your mind that chants. Identify yourself with the intellect, and learn to observe that the mind is steadily chanting. At this time you will experience a deep peace and joy welling up within.

You will notice after some days of practice that the mind can chant very freely but at the same time wander into worldly fields of activity. At such moments demand that your intellect control the mind, and continue to chant at an increased pitch, but mentally. After some ten or fifteen minutes you may start to feel a growing mental fatigue. Stop at this point, allowing all the noises in the mind to die down with the last chant.

At that moment you may experience a God-like peace and divine silence descending on your heart, arousing feelings of supreme joyousness. Remain in that state for as long as you can. This state of silence, at its highest intensity, is a state of transcendence of the mind and intellect. It will take some time before you master this absorption into silence, because of your old habits of always holding thought-currents in your mind. As soon as you come to that state of no-thought, you will automatically and unconsciously initiate the flow of new strands of thought! Don't try by force to lengthen this no-thought state of mind. Let it come of its own spontaneity, else you may create suppressions.

The longer the interval between the moment you have stopped chanting and the moment when your first thought-current begins, the more you will experience the positive quality and vitality of that seemingly empty state. With reference to the usual nonstop rumblings in your mind, the quieter mental atmosphere at this moment can be described as empty. But with reference to the spirit, this state is not a mere undynamic, empty nonexistence, but is instead All-full Existence.

In the next chapter we will see how this hollow emptiness is to be charged with a positive Knowledge of the spirit.

The Positive Mind

20

If a house has been deserted for a long time, it has naturally fallen into disrepair, and every nook and corner of it gets soon covered with dust and cobwebs. On entering it, a moldy smell assails your nostrils. If you want to make it habitable once again, you will have to open all doors and windows to ventilate it, scrub it from roof to floor, whitewash it, paint it, repair it where necessary. Still it won't be fit for comfortable living. You will have to fit it intelligently with furnishings of good taste and decor to render it comfortable and inviting.

The removal of unwanted lumber, dust, and cobwebs is but half the process of making the deserted house habitable once again. The other half consists of bringing in new objects calculated to give comfort to the occupants. Similarly, one cannot secure in the mind a new set of positive qualities before the negativities are removed. Our minds, which are at present encrusted with unhealthy poisons from untold years of neglect, must of necessity first be cleaned to make them fit abodes for divinity. Animal passions, blinding anger, and greed must be drained away. Negative values must be shed through consistent efforts at being good, and the mind replenished with positive values of truthfulness, love, and beauty. Then alone can divinity come to dwell within.

Spirituality is the technique you need to accomplish this change. Actual achievement must be preceded by firm determination. Once begun, this process gathers momentum; thereafter, constant vigilance ensures smooth transformation.

Merely negating the outer world or our known weaknesses cannot by itself lead to upliftment. Negation is not growth, although it prepares the ground for growth. In the ground thus prepared, the desired seeds must be sown and diligently watered.

Fructification follows as a matter of course. If seeds of positive qualities are not implanted, undesirable weeds will shoot up to create a jungle instead of a garden. Blind, unintelligent negation unaccompanied by assiduous assertion of positive values may lead the seeker into a despairing vacuum. The mind is suppressed without being simultaneously elated with positive qualities. A suppressed mind is potentially dangerous. In an unguarded moment it may burst and like dynamite blast the entire structure of progress. The seeker who merely negates soon reaches a state of impotence and inertia. His is a living death; his wan smile denotes no victory whatever. Hasty, though enthusiastic, seekers have often unwittingly landed onto this suicidal path. For want of cultivation of positive qualities of the mind, many gallant seekers after years of impressive practice have felt bogged down or even fallen back into the mire from which they had sought to lift themselves. Negation is essential, yet dangerous!

A positive mind does, rather than just refrains from doing. Suppression of desires is replaced by positive desirelessness. A positive mind does not merely eschew jealousy, but rejoices in the prosperity of others; it does not merely refrain from hating, but it loves; it does not just tolerate, but it forgives; it does not merely desist from telling lies, but it always speaks the truth; it is not only free of greed, but it is generous. A positive mind is poised in peace, free from delusions, seeking the good of all and flowing with unbroken love for everyone. A mind thus cultivated gets attuned to the One and consequently becomes the master of all situations, never a slave. All religions, therefore, prescribe a list of Do's along with a list of Don't's.

Recharge the Mind

21

Ordinarily the mind is active. It is its nature to be forever unsteady. It cannot remain, even for a moment, without entertaining one thought or another. In the above discussions, we analyzed techniques whereby the mind can be made to function in a field we have chosen for it.

When the mind functions exclusively in a given field, it becomes highly potent, obedient, and vital. We saw how we can order the mind to halt its chanting, leaving its only field of occupation at that moment.[1] In the moment of vital silence that follows, the mind is at its most dynamic, though compared to our ordinary experiences, we might consider the silence to be "empty." Some misunderstand this silent moment of extreme dynamism as an impotent interval of emptiness or of nonexistence. It is not so. Actually, these vital moments alone can live enduringly and create the Eternal. An average member of modern society cannot easily appreciate this assertion of Vedanta. He knows only a world limited by time, space, and causality—a world whose existence is expressed in and through its multiple objects and happenings.

However, even if we observe the world of objects, we can find that this assertion of Vedanta is perfectly true. As an example, let us try to see the world as it was some millions of years ago. At the time of its early formation, we know life on this planet was dominated by two great factors. On the one hand, there was a vast turbulence—volcanoes, huge and terrifying, vomiting their lava from inexhaustible fires in the earth's core. On the other hand, there was the miniscule evidence of protoplasm—microscopic, invisible to the naked eye, fragile, quiet, yet vital—lying along the water's

---

[1] In Chapter 19.

edge. Where would you have placed your faith—in the turbulent volcanoes or in the quiet, microscopic dots of throbbing protoplasm?

Had we been the observers in those ancient days, few of us would have voted for the protoplasm. Few of us would have imagined that it would assert itself against the violent forces of volcanoes or the shattering oscillations of repeated earthquakes. We know now what emerged from this fragile matter—life, spirit, artists, scientists, saints, and prophets.

The vital moments of silence that we reach in meditation are eternal islands of Truth among endless billows of life's activities, temptations, struggles, and desires. We are not accustomed to this inner silence. We are like foreigners, self-exiled from our own real nature of peace and serenity. We do not know how to delve into this silent, vibrant existence and translate it into a way of living at once divine and omnipotent.

When we are completely and totally in that state of silence, we are in the realm of Truth. In fact, there is nothing more for a human being to achieve. In that moment of silence—if we can consciously gain entrance into the message of its vitality and come to live its full glory—we would be living the very destiny of Godhood. Unfortunately for many of us, when we reach there, we don't know it for what it is and fail to understand our experience: that it is, indeed, the experience of the Supreme and the Eternal.

I meet a man in a public park and fall into a long and pleasant chat with him. That individual may be the very one whom I have been anxious to meet for a long time; yet, unless I have the knowledge that the man whom I have been talking to in the park is the same individual I have been searching for, I will not, in that experience of accidental meeting, gain the real satisfaction. Similarly, though in that silent moment in meditation we may be experiencing the absolute Self within us, we do not feel the consummate satisfaction of the experience, because we do not know: "This is That."[2] With Knowledge (jñāna), this silent experience starts to give us the joy that it actually contains. It is in this sense that the scriptures declare that liberation can never be had without Knowledge.

It then becomes our duty to charge our mind with the exact identity and nature of this "zero point," which otherwise may be

---

[2] That this self is the absolute Self.

misunderstood as a void. Once we understand that this vital moment is pregnant with potentialities, we will come to experience, more and more, the real nature of the Self, which is *Brahman*, the All-Self.

With this idea in mind, when you have reached that silent moment in your meditation, before entertaining any other thought, either chant or bring to mind any of the following verses, losing yourself fully in the meaning. Written by the famed Vedantin Shankaracharya, these verses are known as "The Song of Supreme Knowledge" (*Brahma Jñānāvali*).

> Unattached, unattached,
> Unattached am I, again and again.
> By nature eternal existence-knowledge-bliss am I.
> I am, that am I,
> The irreducible, immortal, endless factor.

> Eternal, ever pure, ever liberated am I,
> Formlessness my only form.
> By nature I am an all-pervading, homogeneous mass
>   of bliss.
> I am, That am I,
> The irreducible, immortal, endless factor.

> Eternal, countless, formless,
> Irreducible am I.
> By nature bliss am I.
> I am, that am I,
> The irreducible, immortal, endless factor.

> By nature I am pure light,
> And I revel in my own Self.
> I am by nature of unbroken bliss.
> I am, that am I,
> The irreducible, immortal, endless factor.

> By nature I am the innermost light of intelligence.
> I am the peace that lies beyond Nature.
> By nature I am ever-abiding bliss.
> I am, that am I,
> The irreducible, immortal, endless factor.

I am the supreme Truth that lies beyond all other truths.
I am supreme Shiva,[3] ever across the frontiers of
    delusion.
I am the supreme light.
I am, that am I,
The irreducible, immortal, endless factor.

I am different from the multiple names and forms.
Pure Knowledge alone is my form.
I am imperishable, by nature joyous.
I am, that am I,
The irreducible, immortal, endless factor.

In me there is no *māyā*,
Nor its effects, such as the body.
I am of the form of Self-effulgence.
I am, that am I,
The irreducible, immortal, endless factor.

I am of the form of the inner ruler,
Anvil-like, changeless, and all-pervading.
I am in my real nature none other than the supreme Self.
I am, that am I,
The irreducible, immortal, endless factor.

I am by nature a witness of all pairs of opposites.
Motionless, most ancient.
I am the eternal witness of everything.
I am, that am I,
The irreducible, immortal, endless factor.

I am a mass of Consciousness.
I am a mass of Knowledge, too.
I am a nondoer, I am a nonenjoyer.
I am, that am I,
The irreducible, immortal, endless factor.

---

[3] Shiva is God in the aspect of Destroyer, one of the Hindu Trinity. He destroys the delusion of impurity and limitation in us and reveals to us the seat of pure Auspiciouness.

In my real nature I need no other foundation,
But at once am I, in my real nature, the foundation for
    all.
I am by nature self-contented, self-sufficient.
I am, that am I,
The irreducible, immortal, endless factor.

I am beyond the three agonies.[4]
I am different from the three bodies.[5]
I am the witness of the three states.[6]
I am, that am I,
The irreducible, immortal, endless factor.

There are only two things in the whole world,[7]
And they are between themselves the most contrary.
Of them the Subject is the supreme Truth,
And the object is mere delusion.
Thus roars Vedanta.

Through knowledge and repeated discrimination
One comes to realize that one is but a witness.
Established in the "I am witness" Consciousness
Lives the liberated wise man.
Thus roars Vedanta.

Pots, cups, saucers
Are all in essence but the mud from which they were
    shaped.
So too, the entire world of phenomenal objects
Is nothing but the supreme Truth.
Thus roars Vedanta.

Brahman is Truth; the world of objects and beings is
    false,
And the ego is itself, in fact, nothing but *Brahman* alone.

---

[4] Subjective, phenomenal, and cosmic.
[5] The gross, the subtle, and the causal.
[6] The waking, the dreaming, and the sleeping.
[7] The Subject and the object, the Enjoyer and the enjoyed, the Experiencer and the experienced, the Seer and the seen.

That by which this Truth is known is the truest science,
The science of all sciences.
Thus roars Vedanta.

Within am I light, without am I light,
Deep within the depth of myself am I light,
Beyond the beyond![8]
Light of lights, the Self-effulgent light,
The Self's own light, Shiva am I,
Auspiciousness am I.

---

[8] God, the Cause, is "beyond" the world, the effect; and the Reality is "beyond the beyond," as God and the world are both but expressions of the one supreme Self.

The Secret of Success 22

Education is nurtured on books, associations, and practices. Culture is nourished through study of, and reflection upon, books on culture; association and companionship with cultured society; and appreciation and practice of cultural perfections in thought, word, and speech. Meditation can best be maintained and nourished by our intelligent study of the scriptures, by our companionship with the good, and by our conscientious and deliberate living of a life of meditation.

Some seekers expect and even demand shortcuts to perfection. Unfortunately, there are no such shortcuts, although traders in religion and black marketeers in spiritualism would promise such "instant" perfection to anybody approaching them. Such false promises are often found lavishly printed and freely and noisily published.

To demand a shortcut in spirituality is to demand a falsehood. No guru can promise you shortcuts. The shortest cut is to cut the ego in two and make a tunnel to the kingdom of Truth that lies within!

Almost all possible difficulties on the path, arising because of the psychological maladjustments of the personality, are removed by the regular practice of the processes advised. However great a medication may be, the disease will not be cured just because the patient has procured the medicine. She has to take it in small doses for a period of time and allow her system to digest it. The medicine must become part and parcel of her physical structure. Similarly, techniques, methods, and theories can never help us cure ourselves of the disease arising from our faults of personality—unless we are ready to make slow but steady renunciation of the false and develop the true.

Thus, all that the novice in meditation can do is to be sincere and regular in practicing daily meditation. Live all the hours of the day in consciousness of the Divine and the Eternal. Play the game of life, play whatever part you have been called upon to play, but never forget your greater mission in life and the ultimate goal you want to achieve.

Through diligent practice and sincere pursuit of the nobler values of life, get yourself more and more attached to the higher and nobler in life. The extent of your success in attaching the mind to the nobler values of life will be directly proportional to the amount of detachment you gain from the low and the vicious. Detachment from "here" is attachment to "there." Progress is not possible without renunciation. Life itself is a progression from birth to death, from moment to moment. Each moment is renounced so that we may live the coming moment. Unless we are ready to leave the immediate spot on which we are standing, we cannot take a step forward. The only known method for climbing a ladder is to leave the lower rung and get on to the next higher one.

In the inward march toward the goal of perfection, we must also renounce at every step. We must renounce false values of selfishness, vanity, greed, and passions by acquiring their opposite good qualities. Whoever practices this diligently will enjoy immediate progress, surprisingly sudden and full. All obstructions in our spiritual path are obstructions put up by ourselves. The more we live the right values, the more we will succeed in our meditation. The technique of right living is amply explained in the Upanishads, and nowhere so well as in the *Katha Upaniṣad*[1] with its elaborate description of the technique in the analogy of the body-chariot.

Many unintelligent students of spirituality, in their attempt to understand the scriptural significance through mere book study, come to the hasty conclusion that the Vedantic technique of meditation cannot help an individual in life. A few even strive to prove that a meditator who practices regularly is someone heading for sure failure in life. Vedanta is not in any sense of the term a pessimistic negation of life. It is a healthy philosophy that promotes the growth and happiness of the human being both in his indi-

---

[1] Refer to Swami Chinmayananda's commentary on the *Katha Upaniṣad* Chapter I, Section III, Verses 3-9.

vidual and in his communal life and points a way to reach the Beyond, but surely *in and through life.*

The greater the amount of concentration that a seeker can apply in his everyday life, the greater will be his success in meditation. Anyone who practices meditation correctly will necessarily gain in all efforts at concentration. Again, as he develops in meditation, he gains more in his ethical and moral perfection and in his devotion to the Lord, which must necessarily give him a greater amount of intellectual poise and mental peace. Anyone who has thus grown rich in concentration, intellectual poise, mental peace, and integrity of character will most surely succeed in any walk of life and reach realms beyond the purview of the average person.

Thus viewed, meditation becomes a true education, a secret preparation to face the world of unsteady circumstances and evanescent glories. True meditation can fashion out of any ordinary person an incomparable genius. The stories of the great sages of the world all tell us that they often had nothing much to claim for their general education; many of them enjoyed none of the circumstances conducive to achieving anything spectacular; yet they grew to their brilliant stature through their practice of meditation. Ultimately they became immortal people of wisdom. Even if one saint or sage from the past could thus redeem himself from the limitations of the mortal and raise himself above the average in his own lifetime, every one of us has the right to claim this privilege as our sacred heritage. Meditate and grow.

Inward Expansion

23

Our knowledge of things in the world is purely relative. An object viewed from different angles is experienced by us differently. Thus, a stupendous redwood tree seen from the top of a distant hill will look like a meager mushroom growth; but as we descend from the peak, the tree changes in our perception, and when we finally reach its foot we recognize it in all its mighty girth. The tree remaining the same, from different points of observation it seems to have different dimensions and impresses us differently. Our conceptions of distance, time, and size are all relative.

Living as we are in the delusory misconception that we are the body, mind, and intellect, we have the false notion that they are real and substantial. If we move a little farther away from them into higher realms of imagination or spiritual experience, we shall begin to experience the idea that the ego-sense in us is an insignificant and hollow nothing.

In order to perceive this insignificance of our self-asserting egoistic arrogance, we have to step away from the ego for a moment and in our detachment learn to observe it through the microscope of pure discrimination. Our permanent proximity to the ego has given our own ego-myth a far greater importance than it deserves. Let us examine this more closely.

We all feel that we are irrevocably real and unquestionably substantial, as individuals in our own homes. But let us analyze this further. My home is denoted by a number on the door among many such doors on the street; my street is a road or byroad off a main road; the main road is one of the many roads in the city; and the city is a mere spot on the map of the district. The district, again, is a jot in the state; the state is a fraction of the country; the country is part of a continent; and many continents make up this globe, the world.

We know that the world is one of innumerable heavenly bodies that constitute our galaxy, each one separated from the others by billions and trillions of miles. We are told that there are millions of such galaxies in the universe. This total space, with all its many galaxies, is but an insignificant portion of the total Reality. Therefore, in the context of this universe, what importance, significance, substantiality, or relevance can I claim for my numbered house?

In this house, what space do I occupy? There may be five rooms in the house, but all that I occupy at any given time is a fraction of a chair in one corner of one room! Yet, how stupidly arrogant and self-assertive I can be, as though besides myself there were nothing more superior, nothing more important. In reality, how microscopic is my structure and personality when compared with the Lord of Lords, the supreme Reality, the All-Pervading!

Having come to this misunderstanding that I am a tiny, limited body-mind-intellect equipment, conditioned by matter, I have become the worm-man that I am. The rediscovery of myself to be nothing other than the limitless, homogeneous mass of Consciousness, absolute and eternal, is the only remedy for curing the sorrows caused by my ignorance of my own real nature.

Expand inwardly. Grow to your full stature. You can achieve growth and expansion only in and through meditation. You shall not rest now with the mere chanting of *Om* in your mind. That was a technique that you followed in order to learn to talk with the mind. The practice of mental *japa* has given you the necessary training to make your mind obedient to your commands.

Instead of concentrating your entire attention in making the mind chant *Om* and listening to the sound of *Om* as though rising from the heart or the mind or even from a point farther down, your next attempt will be in a different direction altogether. You shall continue chanting *Om* as sincerely as ever before, but you will no longer strive to note the source of its rising. Now you will watch the *Om*-vibration rising from the depth of yourself, growing and merging into an ever-increasing peace and joy. Let this atmosphere of *Om*-vibrations grow and expand into the uncharted extensions of the Absolute. Get yourself reduced to nothingness in the ever-growing atmosphere of the *Om*-substance.

If you reach this state of expansion wherein you see your ego-self as a speck of nothingness in relation to the Absolute that you are in your true nature, you will grow into an atmosphere of pure Intelligence wherein the entire universe that exists in space becomes, in your spiritual vision, but a momentary dream in one of Its folds.

PART
Three

Aids to
Meditation

A Review of
Procedure

24

To review the key points of the technique of meditation:

1. *Seat.* Set aside a clean space or small room for meditation. Sit on a soft, flat cushion or a blanket folded in four.

2. *Posture.* If you find it comfortable, sit in a legs-folded position, with the right leg over the left leg, a position that will give you a maximum base. If you find this position a strain, sit in any other comfortable position, but always keep your vertebral column erect, thrusting slightly forward at the pelvic region. Place your palms in your lap; keep your right palm over the left.

3. *Thought-massage.* Relax your body and start mentally massaging the various parts of the body—neck, shoulders, upper arm, lower arm, hands, chest, abdomen, trunk, back, thighs, knees, legs, and feet. Let the mind inspect each muscle, releasing its stiffness and tension. At this point the withdrawal of your attention from the disturbances of the physical body should be complete.

4. *Thought-parade.* Allow any thoughts that have already formed in your mind to rise to the surface and exhaust themselves as you identify with your intellect and detachedly witness each thought rising and passing away. Be careful not to initiate any new thoughts at this time. At the completion of this step, the immediate agitations in the mind will have dissipated, making your mind available for meditation.

5. *Contemplating the Lord's form.* Fix your gaze upon the symbol of the Lord of your heart, Whom you have chosen for your contemplation, and surrender to Him demanding in love His help, guidance, and grace.

6. *Om-chanting by the mouth.* With your eyes resting on the symbol of the Lord, begin to chant *Om* audibly and vibrantly from deep within. Let the *Om* vibrations grow and expand around you

to form an enveloping atmosphere. Let the vibrations unfold themselves into ever-widening ripples and continue chanting vigorously and sincerely.

7. Om-*chanting by the mind.* Gently close your eyes, stop the audible chanting, and begin to chant *Om* silently with the mind. If your tongue and throat strive to pronounce the chant, first relax your tongue on the floor of the mouth and then mentally control the chanting that is still striving to rise in the throat. Let the chant be totally in your mind. Identify yourself with the intellect and watch the mind chanting.

8. *Thoughtless state.* Put a sudden stop to the chanting as though someone had shouted "Stop!" If you find this difficult, resume your chanting, chanting ever louder and louder in the mind, and when you have reached the peak, slowly reduce the tone of this mental roar until it becomes a mere mental whisper. Then allow the whisper to dissolve and disappear into silence. When you reach the thoughtless state, hold on to it as long as you comfortably can. As soon as the first thought rises up to disturb the peace, chant any of the stanzas from Shankaracharya's *Brahma Jñānāvali.*[1] Repeat this process as many as three times at each sitting.

---

[1] Quoted in Chapter 21.

Hints for Taming the Mind

25

In the last few chapters you learned some details of how to go about meditation and gained some rough knowledge of a sure technique. However, in time you will find out that in spite of the techniques and the underlying wisdom, the mind still continues to wander. To hold the mind until it is an integrated whole becomes a painful and difficult task. This inner struggle is symbolized in the battle portrayed in the *Mahābhārata*, and it is an eternal one.[1] This inner struggle is the price that we must pay for the eternal reward of liberation.

We have seen that the mind is a product of the impressions we have gathered in our lives, from beginningless time up to today. In all of our incarnations, we have been living endless experiences, and the experience of each moment has left an impression in the mental sheath. Goaded by these impressions, memories, and desires, we develop the conviction that we possess an irresistible mind that is wild and surging, carrying us endlessly hither and thither. Tossed in its agitations, we feel shattered in our attempts at meditation.

When the good and the bad meet face to face, tension and activity are always present. It is an eternal law. We can never mentally get away from these two opposing forces, and when we identify with them we suffer the consequent dissipations. At one moment we identify with the good in us, and then feel unhappy because, in spite of ourselves, we feel tempted to act in a vicious,

---

[1] The *Mahābhārata* is an ancient epic poem reputedly written by Veda Vyasa. Consisting of some 110,000 verses, the epic includes the famed *Bhagavad Gītā* and depicts the bitter dynastic war between the Pandavas and the Kauravas.

negative way. At another moment, in spite of satanic inclinations, we succeed at doing something good and feel elated. The tension between God and Satan within the seeker is eternal. But if the seeker gives himself up to the supreme control of the divine Charioteer, even disaster will spell success for him.[2]

The mind is the challenge and the threat that faces every meditator. The mind of its nature is ever running into its chosen, instinct-driven ruts. The meditator's attempt must be to bundle up all the wasteful channels of the mind and direct the thought-flow through one chosen channel. A thorough knowledge of the mind's strategies becomes absolutely essential if we hope to hold the mind to one point of concentration and win the war against our lower self.

The following methods may be employed to gain control over the mind—not all of them at once, but one at a time. If you discover that you have used the wrong tool, change the instrument to win your moment-to-moment victories.

1. *Bring the mind back forcefully.* Whenever your mind runs off, become aware of it and at once strive to bring it back to meditation by force if need be. This method is, in fact, the means and the goal in one.

2. *Be conscious of what you are doing.* When you pray or meditate, be fully conscious of what you are doing. The mind that wanders is a mind that has left its aim of concentration; invariably we go off with the mind, not recognizing for a long time that the mind has indeed wandered. Therefore, constant alertness is essential.

It is for the purpose of keeping fully conscious of our activity that we have congregational prayers, chiming of bells, burning of incense, beautiful lights, and symbols of the Lord. Also, every religion insists that we cleanse ourselves before prayer and prepare a clean place for our worship. If the temple of God is in a place no different than the waiting room of a busy bus depot, we shall find as much peace and concentration in the temple as at the depot.

3. *Chant with the eyes open.* Even after the physical surroundings are properly arranged, you may find that when you try to meditate, subtle causes arising from the inner world try to sabotage

---

[2] The parallel in the *Bhagavad Gītā* of the *Mahābhārata* holds firm: Arjuna's charioteer in the thick of the civil war between the Kauravas and Pandavas is Lord Krishna Himself. With Him at the reins, Arjuna succeeds in leading the good forces to victory over the evil ones.

your efforts. Your loves, hates, hopes, desires, and passions dirty your inner world, and, propelled by them, your mind flies off on a tangent. These wanderings are held off by singing the glories of the Lord with your eyes open. At this point you can easily deceive yourself—just as more than ninety percent of religionists all over the world do. They make a great show of their devotion, exhibiting their rituals and various paraphernalia attached to religion. They suffer from exhibitionism rather than being blessed by a true spiritual urge. Sincerity is the secret of success in spiritual seeking.

4. *Give the mind a large but inspiring field to play in.* An uncontrolled mind has developed the habit of wandering into limitless fields. To control such a mind all of a sudden would amount to a degree of suppression, which is not healthy. Thus, all the religions of the world give authorized versions of the history and achievements of its prophets and masters to contemplate upon for steaming up your inspiration. To read such inspiring stories gives your mind a large field to play in, yet a field with some boundaries and one that has an integrating principle underlying every detail, namely, the Lord Himself.

Reducing this relatively large field to a single incident in a master's life and meditating upon it will train the mind to restrain its activities to a more limited area. After this stage, to fix your attention on a chosen symbol of the Lord will still further reduce the area of your attention. Even here, the mind still has a chance to wander among pluralities. In contemplating the form of the Lord, for example, the eye has much to take in: the Lord's feet are not the same as His hips; the lips are different in shape and suggestion from the chest; and the sacred face is still different from the limbs or the trunk.

To aim still nearer to the bull's-eye, you can urge your mind to meditate only upon the face of the Lord. Then, eliminating the various details of the face, to make the mind concentrate steadily on the smile on the lips of the Lord is to reach a high point of concentration through the pleasant path of devotion. But a suggestion of plurality still remains: the lips are two, the upper being different from the lower; and again, a sense of plurality exists between the lips and their smile! With a final effort you should then strive to negate the lips and meditate upon the smile alone. Anyone who tries this will realize that to meditate upon the smile is to live the smile and its voiceless message of divine bliss.

In all these activities of reducing your field of concentration, your success will depend entirely upon the amount of love you can bring to bear in a meditative mood of all-surrendering, total devotion.

5. *Persuade the mind lovingly.* Consider your mind with an attitude of motherly botheration, full of love-prompted anxiety. Loving persuasion is one of the most common methods of mothers in controlling a child bent for mischief. To persuade the mind to realize the glories of meditation as its highest vocation should be your daily preoccupation. The more you are convinced of the benefits that you can gain in meditation, the more you will find that your mind settles down peacefully to meditation.

6. *Lure the mind with promises; kindle its curiosity.* Sometimes a mother will offer her child something tangible to win his attention away from a particular field of indulgence. Upon finding the child ransacking her drawers, the mother might say, "Come here, baby. I have something for you. I've been keeping it for you for several days. If you come here, I'll show it to you." Upon hearing this, the child readily leaves his mischief and runs in curiosity to his mother. Similarly, when the mind is wandering in its usual fields of agitation, you can cajole it back by repeating to yourself the blissful experience that the great masters have acquired through meditation. The curiosity of the mind will be kindled, and, for its own satisfaction, it will for the time being at least come back to apply itself to meditation.

7. *Promise the mind freedom from control at a later time.* Again, a mother's loving tactics can be employed. To lure him away from a present mischief, the mother might promise her child a much ampler field for "mischief" at a later period of time: "If you take your nap now, I'll take you to the park afterward where you can play on the swings until supper." The child weighs the pros and cons of the proposition and finds it profitable to renounce the mischief, take a nap, and look forward to an afternoon in the park.

During meditation, your mind may wander to worry over domestic or business problems, over the international situation, or over its own weaknesses. A diligent seeker can persuade such a mind to stick to meditation by promising it a free ride into these fields of thought later—say, after lunch. This concession must be given only on strict conditions: "I'll let you wander freely among your pet worries after lunch *if* you give me your total cooperation in meditation." Without fail, you will experience that the mind, after a moment's hesitation, becomes supple and comes back to play the tune that you want it to play.

8. *Reprimand the mind and execute your threat.* There are moments when even the best of mothers feels that the child needs a little bit of cane treatment. At such moments—and they certainly must be very rare—the mother not only threatens the child, but executes the threat if she is not obeyed. In sheer fright, the child quickly gets over his extremely wrong tendencies.

Similarly, you must also on occasion severely reprimand the mind and faithfully execute the threats you hold out for its serious crimes. The only whip that can directly reach the mind is starvation or fasting. When you detect that the mind is uncontrollable and behaves as a bull, urge it to behave properly; but if it still persists in being wild, show it the rod, promising a complete fast for the next twenty-four hours. On wintry days you can also punish the mind most severely by prescribing a cold shower if it doesn't behave.

Do not overdo this method. A healthy mind can be had only in a healthy body. If the body gets too weak, the mind will become more and more fatigued, and a fatigued mind cannot toe the line of severe self-discipline. Another thing to watch in this strategy is to avoid becoming too lenient with the mind after passing a judgment of condemnation. After prescribing the maximum punishment, you may succumb to a wise-after-the-event mood and sympathize too leniently with your mind. Thus, having punished the mind with a twenty-four-hour fast, you may become so lenient as to stuff yourself with substitutes of fruits and milk, thereby almost overfeeding both body and mind.

The mind is made up of the subtle aspects of the food that we consume; thus, denial of food is almost denial of the mind's own nourishment. If instead of ordinary food, the mind gets as "punishment" fruits and milk, you will find the mind repeating the same acts that you intended to erase with your punishment in the first place. Once having taken the decision to punish the mind, you must not, on any score, become sentimental and yield to the temptation of easing the sentence.

No intelligent mother will overpunish her child, for experience proves that overpunishment is as detrimental to the child's independent growth as is overindulgence. Overpunishing will make the mind controlled, but ineffectual and impotent; such a dead mind is useless for higher meditation.

9. *Watch the mind with a critical eye.* The most effective punishment for the mind is for you to remain as though apart from the mind, and with a critical eye watch its meaningless somersaults. When a mother finds that her child is uncontrollable in spite of all previous tactics, she stands back and merely watches the child at his mischief with a sad look. The child steals a few glances at the mother and, reading the sorrow in her face, comes to his senses. He feels ashamed of himself, stops his misbehavior, and comes to hug at the mother's skirts, demanding a little special attention. At this moment, no intelligent mother will start scolding, but will attend to the child's wishes, which are, in fact, no different from her own.

When the mind is uncontrollably agitated and runs about wildly, you can identify yourself with your intellect and watch the mind with sympathetic criticism. The mind may still wander for some time, but when it realizes that it is directly under the observation of a disinterested but critical intellect, it becomes, as it were, self-conscious and ashamed of itself and retires from its questionable vocation to apply itself to meditation. This technique is called in the scriptures of Vendanta the technique of witnessing the mind (*sākṣi-bhāva*).

Any one of the above methods should answer your problems at a given moment. A diligent practitioner will discover new methods to circumvent all novel mischiefs of the mind. In all these practices, the most important factor is a deep sense of sincerity, a great conviction born of faith and understanding, and a hardy sense of seeking, at once adventurous and revolutionary. Without these noble qualities of the head and the heart, nothing can be expected of your spiritual practices.

To wait for these qualities to descend upon you from the Heavens or to hope to earn them by pickpocketing a guru is like waiting for somebody who has not yet been born to come and feed you.

Strive hard. Act diligently. Meditate regularly. Discriminate continuously. Be good. Be kind, tolerant, merciful, and all-loving. Eradicate weaknesses, steadily growing in your inner strength. Keep *brahmacarya*, good company, and good health. Even at the point of death renounce dishonesty, deception, lust, and passions. And meditate.

Meditate, meditate, and meditate. This is the only true path to perfection.

Keeping a
Spiritual Diary

Even after following all the prescribed steps faithfully, you may run into obstructions in your efforts at meditation. In almost all cases where a seeker complains of lack of progress, it is because his subtle body has grown grosser. Do not be misled into thinking that your lack of progress is because of "destiny" or "a bad day" or the withdrawal of God's or your guru's grace! During an unconscious moment of relaxation, the sensuous world has invaded your inner world through the sense organs and brought forth from your subconscious mind the lower tendencies. The only way out is to gather up your strength and fight out the battle with your baser tendencies.

In order to protect the growing spiritual wealth in you and not suffer the sorrow of setbacks, it may help to post twenty "soldiers" around you, in the form of twenty questions to put to yourself at the end of each day's activities. Keep track of the questions and answers in the form of a spiritual diary that you keep strictly and continuously for three months, *but never for more than six months at a stretch.* You must not let yourself become habituated to diary-writing. At any time that you feel a setback in your spiritual growth, take up the diary again for a week. It is the experience of many masters and thousands of seekers that this diary-keeping is the sovereign remedy for spiritual fervor turned into sour skepticism.

The following are the twenty items that constitute your diary. The list is compiled to suit all temperaments. Select fifteen items out of the twenty and pursue them diligently. Enter the items as heads for fifteen columns, and indicate each day your report on yourself under each category. At the end of the month, study the chart you have made to determine the schedule of your progress or decline for that month. (See page 177 for a sample form.)

1. *How many hours did I sleep?* Normally six hours of sleep are sufficient for a quiet-living spiritual seeker.

2. *When did I get up from bed?* You should be out of bed between 4:30 and 6:00 a.m. The early morning's quiet will assist you in your spiritual evolution. The great masters have found, from their own personal experience, that this part of the day is most beneficial for spiritual practice. In the early stages, you may need an alarm clock to awaken you. If you find yourself being too sleepy after getting up, let a brisk shower freshen you up.

3. *How long did I practice concentration?* Begin with small doses, and increase the period of concentration slowly and steadily.

4. *What religious books am I now reading?* Reading the lives of the great masters and their declarations of Truth in a spirit of inquiry will greatly help you in thinking intelligently. In reading such books, do not be content with their story content alone. All such stories have deep symbolic and philosophic significance, and your aim should be to unravel the deeper meanings.

5. *For how long was I in companionship with the good (satsang)?* Satsang here does not mean merely attending prayer meetings and religious discourses. Once you have developed the spirit of inquiry, you will automatically seek out friends interested in discussing religious topics with you. Where such friends are not available, good books will serve as good company; discover companionship with them.

6. *For how long did I engage myself in disinterested service* (karma yoga)? Any act of service, performed in a spirit of detachment, will further the growth of the noble qualities of love, tolerance, mercy, and so on. Learn to serve Him through the people you are helping.

7. *How many mālās (rosaries) of* japa *did I perform?* One *mālā* consists of 108 beads, with a mantra chanted at the turning of each bead. In order to do *japa* effectively, you must strive as far as possible to exclude all extraneous thoughts from the mind during the period of *japa* practice.

8. *How many Upanishad mantras did I read?* Read only a little each day, but digest what you have read and allow your mind to reflect over the great truths behind the words of the mantras.

9. *How many mantras did I write?* Mantra-writing is the easiest way of fixing your concentration. Keep a separate notebook for this purpose, and regularly write about a page of your chosen mantra. While writing the mantra, do not speak or look around, nor move away from the work until the allotted amount is finished. This

exercise will aid your concentration immensely, since you soak your mind with the ideal suggested by the mantra as you whisper and write: the hand is writing the mantra, the eyes are seeing the mantra, the mouth is softly chanting the mantra, and the ears are listening to the mantra. The mind thus becomes easily single-pointed.

10. *How many hours did I observe silence?* Keeping silence does not mean expressing all your thoughts in relation to the outside world by making signs. If you do so, your mind will be entertaining thoughts that relate to the objective world. The aim is to withdraw one's attention to the inner world of the spirit.

11. *How many days did I fast?* Fasting here does not mean abstaining from food continuously for long periods of time, such as 21 or 41 days. Fast regularly—once a month, once a week, or once a fortnight.

12. *What did I give away in charity?* Giving here means giving in thought, cash, or kind.

13. *How many lies did I tell and with what self-punishment?* A lie is something uttered against your conscience with a view of obtaining some advantage for yourself. During the act of lying, you will all the time be conscious of uttering something against your natural inclinations in order to surmount a real or imagined difficulty. Such conflicts will haunt you after the lie has been told and will become a wall of China in your spiritual practice. Do not allow yourself to console yourself by saying that the lie was small and did not affect anyone detrimentally. In all events, lying disturbs your mental poise. If you tell a lie, give yourself severe punishment, such as fasting or increasing the period of daily silence.

14. *How many times was I angry, and how long did each attack of anger last?* Anger arises out of nonfulfillment of your desires. Array the forces of tolerance, mercy, sympathy, and understanding of the weakness in yourself and in others in order to win a victory over anger.

15. *How many hours did I spend in useless company?* In all spiritual practices you should attempt to see yourself as a child who desires to come home after having stayed away for a time, charmed by some pleasant attraction elsewhere. In spiritual practice, this coming home is possible only if you scrupulously avoid useless company, thus creating a proper atmosphere for your inner work.

16. *How many times did I fail in* brahmacarya? Remember, *brahmacarya* means self-control in all areas—eating, talking, sex,

and any other indulgences. Self-control within bounds is the safest rule.

17. *What virtues am I developing consciously?* For a month at a time, take to the cultivation of a single noble quality, such as love, tolerance, or kindness.

18. *What evil quality am I trying to eradicate?* Become conscious of thoughts that hold you down and slow your spiritual progress. Negative qualities are like a millstone tied around your neck while you are trying to swim. You have to snap the cord, let the weight sink, rise to the surface of the water, and swim to the shore. You must diagnose your own malady and find its proper cure.

19. *How many times did I fail in controlling an evil habit, and with what punishment?* Punishment here may be dealt out similarly as in paragraph 13, above.

20. *When did I go to bed?* Simply enter the time of retiring.

PART Four

Hasten Slowly

Each day before meditation read one chapter in this section in a whispering tone. After your meditation, instead of immediately allowing your mind to explode into fields of activity, allow it to glide slowly into the vigor of the daily routine: again read the same chapter, as before, in a whispering tone.

Consider that the words you read are advice given by your own intellect to your *own* erring mind and indisciplined body. It is an inner sermon heard by your own mind and body equipment.

I have found this practice to be very helpful for the majority of early meditators. Also, since the early morning hours provide the most impressionable time, the mind gets impregnated with these ideas, so that the seeker's character unfoldment is spectacular and complete.

Progress-Halting Ruts 27

The cruelest periods for a sincere seeker during his spiritual life are the moments before the final divine experience. The pathetic anguish felt by him on the path is called "the dark night of the soul." This stage of extreme helplessness, complete disappointment, total dejection, and utter despair—though unavoidable—can be minimized if the seeker, on his meditation-flight to the transcendental, is well equipped and fully trained for this supreme, subjective adventure. It is the unprepared student who falls into unproductive, progress-halting ruts of thought and gets torn in the rising storms within him.

The spiritual literature of Vedanta scatters pointers and signposts throughout its texts to guide the seekers who get stranded on the great path. Silhouetted against the dim light of our enthusiasm, each one of them presents but a vague shape of the pointing hand of the post. Everyone must pursue the pilgrimage in the direction so confidently shown by the unerring words of the Upanishads: all commentaries and explanations, annotations and discourses are attempts to raise a fluttering candle to the ambiguous crossroad signs left in the scriptures.

Without all the preliminary preparations no one should start on a great pilgrimage. If a traveler does so, it is clear that he has no sincerity or sense of urgency to reach the destination. The vehicle must be properly rigged, the fuel tank filled, the engine well tuned up, and the tools packed before he gets behind the wheel and drives away. The traveler must have the necessary technical knowledge to spot troubles and correct them en route. And as he travels ahead, he must be alert to read the road signs and obey their directions implicitly; at places where he is in doubt, it will always be rewarding to slow down, even stop and get out, meet others on the road, inquire, and ascertain whether he is traveling in the right direction.

For a sincere seeker who is on the way to successful contemplative flights, the pointers in the scriptures are all useful hints to keep him steadily on the path. A successful meditator is one who faithfully keeps to the general plan of action laid down in the sacred texts.

The final peak of success aimed at by a mind in meditation is its own merger into the great silence—into pure Consciousness, which is the matrix behind the entire subtle world of subjective thoughts-and-emotions and the gross realm of objective things-and-beings. The conscious thoughts, in their enlivened vitality, give us the apparent illusion of an individuality, known popularly as the ego (jīva).

The mind is the thought-flow in us. The quality, quantity, and direction of the thoughts in an individual determine the type of flow in him, and consequently it alone decides the worth, the beauty, and the effectiveness of his personality as expressed in life. All the psychiatric treatments doled out today are attempts to jerk the thought-flow of the patient into a harmonious rhythm. But the valleys cut by the long periods of wrong flow have created disturbing patterns of thought-gush in the subject, and he has an irresistible tendency to dash back into the old, familiar stream of thinking and living. A spiritual seeker, to begin with, must therefore learn to initiate new and healthier channels of thought and thereby vividly etch the desired scheme of spiritually conducive mental behavior.

The direction of thoughts in the mind is determined by the peculiar subsurface motivating factors found within the emotional profile of each one of us. These factors are called vāsanās. When we are conscious of their pull, and when we realize that they are—at least some of them—conditioning us and dragging us into incompetence and into futile mental and physical dissipations, we call them "mental hang-ups." All of us have many such hang-ups, and we struggle in vain against them, and ultimately, in our weariness, we come to yield to them. A spiritual seeker must conquer these vāsanās in order to master his mind. Without this mastery over the thought-flow, self-expansion and self-experience are mere hopes, false dreams, empty claims, unprofitable bluffs.

The inner and subtler forces are more powerful than the outer and grosser factors ordering our life and our world, and therefore

1 mixture

the rishis advise us first to learn to conquer, control, and tame the outer equipment of perception—the sense organs. The sense organs are miserable slaves in their own chosen harem of enchanting objects. Remember, it is certainly excusable if the physical sense organs seek to fulfill themselves in the physical objects; for there is always a natural affinity for matter toward matter. But the individual personality should not get involved in them. So long as we live identified with the sense organs and committed to their passions, we can never wean ourselves away from the confusing medley of our riotous sense appetites for sense objects.

In fact, the sense organs cannot function without the mind; and so, by raising the vision of the mind and engaging the mind entertainingly absorbed at a nobler altar of adoration, the sense organs can be clutched off and their dash into the fields of sense objects can be slowed down. Yet, the remedy suggested is, in fact, not available to the raw seeker, because the mind cannot be readily lifted to a greater vision unless the motivating forces functioning in it are purified and controlled.

The force that drives the mind to whip and herd the sense organs into the cesspool of sense objects is the *intellect* and its various schemes for happiness called *desires*. Again, these desires gurgling up in the intellect, poisoning the entire personality, are themselves manifestations of the ultimate source of all conditionings, the motivating urges deep in our unconscious, the *vāsanās*. This level of our personality is called by the rishis the *causal body*, because it is the ultimate determining factor that orders a given type of mind and intellect (*subtle body*) and all behavior on the physical level (*gross body*).

The causal level of our personality—the unconscious depthlayer of our mind—is indicated in the Upanishadic discussions as nescience or ignorance (*avidyā*). Ignorance of our spiritual essence, and its infinite glory and perfection, is the cause for our sense of restlessness, loneliness, and fear, and therefore the intellect desires, the mind agitates for, and the sense organs indulge in the world of sense objects. The sense gratifications bring but more and more fatigue at all levels of the sensuous person, and never a deep, consoling satisfaction. Dissatisfied, the individual's intellect plans yet another desire, and the body sweats and toils again to seek and fulfill it—only to discover the same disconcerting sense of emptiness filling his heart, a painful weight of dissatisfaction crushing him in the end!

Sooner or later we realize that all the wealth acquired, all objects of pleasure procured, all relationships maintained, name and fame gained, work done, achievements accomplished—none of them has any relevance to our inner peace and joy. The entire life then seems an empty struggle, a futile exertion, a meaningless mission.

Thus, the rishis pithily declare that the pangs of our life are all due to our own spiritual ignorance, consisting of the irresistibly compelling urge to love, to acquire, and to enjoy the world around us. The removal of this ignorance is the goal of meditation. With the knowledge (*vidyā*) of the spiritual center, the Self, ignorance is ended. "Seek the Self" is the silent scream of the highest meditation.

On this grand path of spirituality, hasten slowly.

Mental Dancings 28

The entire personality complex is maintained and run by *vāsanās*, and they are generated by our egocentric contacts with the world of objects. In passionate hunger for sense gratification, when our personality runs out in extroverted seeking and clinging to the joys of sense objects, our sensuous *vāsanās* increase in our personality composition. The more numerous these subconscious urges and motivating factors in an individual, the greater grows his or her surge of desires and the more incessant become the devastating agitations in the mind. In such an individual the sense organs cannot remain withdrawn and quiet. They must gallop on toward indulgence in the sense objects that promise but perishable moments of pleasure.

Once a desire is gratified, there is no permanent satisfaction: the gratification only kindles more desires, more thirst. Therefore, the subtle thinkers of the past rightly advised the seekers who are striving to gain mastery over their mind. "Toward all objects give up every trace of attachment. This is the secret means of winning over the mind."[1]

Our attachment to the objects makes the objects powerful, and then the objects come to rule over our mind. If we are seeking to master the mind, we must therefore learn to live without entangling ourselves in the endless meshes of attachments by which the personality gets irretrievably bound to the objects and beings around us.

Thus, when the seeker gets attached to the goal of conquering the mind, all his other fascinations automatically end and completely drop away. The greater his attachments to external objects,

---

[1] From *Bhāgavatam*.

he now realizes, the more wild and uncontrollable his mind. The very goal he has now chosen, the conquest of his mind, helps him to curtail, regulate, control, and ultimately annihilate all his clinging attachments to the world.

We cling only to things that we understand contain some joy for us. Thirst for happiness is natural with every living organism in this universe. The murderer expects happiness for himself after the killing of his enemy; the drunkard believes that his happiness is in his bottle; the devotee finds his happiness in his prayers; the poor, in searching for crumbs, and the rich and the powerful, in trying to gain economic and political domination over the whole world—all are seeking their individual fulfillment in happiness.

This thirst is a built-in urge natural to all thoughtless people. A little quiet contemplation and self-inquiry can reveal that the outer objects do not contain what we are demanding, and that our demand is not really for these objects.

Yet, all of us dissipate our energies in this futile, mad quest, with a quixotic fervor, a consistent foolishness, and a charming idiocy. We refuse to think. When our anxious demand to master the mind reaches its peak, a sincere and deep urgency comes to assert itself to accomplish, as quickly as possible, this release of our individuality from the suicidal tyranny of our own mind. This anxious urgency is called śraddhā. As a seeker cultivates herself and her śraddhā grows in depth, she discovers in herself an endless enthusiasm to put forth any amount of joyous efforts at mastering her mind. Without such a spring of enlivening enthusiasm, the spiritual practice becomes laborious, unrewarding, burdensome, and sooner or later the seeker leaves the field, vanquished and routed by the mind.

Once we generate in our heart a certain amount of this spiritual enthusiasm, we can easily and readily remember our chosen goal constantly. If the constant awareness of the goal is blazing in the highways of our mind, then in our hurried living and the rush of events and happenings we will not, even accidentally, cater to the idle demands of the mind and thus fall again unwillingly into a new set of clinging attachments, expecting happiness from the acquisition of and indulgence in sense objects. The constant remembrance of our goal will serve as a steady warning light, and it will guide us steadily on our pilgrimage through all the day-to-day contentions of the busy, brutal life in the community!

Thus, once *śraddhā*, the sincere urgency for mastering the mind, has manifested in us, spiritual enthusiasm in applying ourselves to its achievement immediately follows; and when this enthusiasm is present, we cannot but steadily remember our determined goal. When a seeker lives thus in the constant remembrance of his ideal to be attained, his concentration naturally grows.

The capacity of the mind to entertain one idea consistently, to the exclusion of all dissimilar thoughts, is called concentration. This single-pointed, mental self-application to an exclusive idea becomes inevitable in a seeker who remembers the goal constantly.

For all our spiritual conquests the forces we employ are those of our single-pointed concentration. But however large our army may be, its strength lies in the education, culture, and discipline of its members. Else the army may win the battle yet lose the war by its own indiscipline and victorious excesses. Similarly, concentration is the secret weapon that we must use to storm the citadel of Truth; but this weapon in an impure heart may convert all its successes into suicidal self-annihilation. Therefore, we must cultivate the ethical and moral virtues side by side. A person rich in these glorious traits alone can use the powers of concentration for the creative programs of mastering the mind.

The values of life that arise in our contact with others in society constitute our strategy and policy, regulating and beautifying all our relationships with others. The rishis of yore experimented with these values. They prescribed the right attitude toward specific types of challenges. Thus, "friendliness toward happy ones, kindness toward unhappy ones, joyous enthusiasm toward the virtuous and the righteous, disregard toward sensuous sinners"[2] are prescribed as the healthy attitudes to be cultivated and maintained by all seekers. In this way we learn to *involve* ourselves with the good, *commit* ourselves to the righteous, and *avoid* all the evil influences of the sinful.

By bringing up our personality in this way, in the midst of the tensions of the competitive marketplace of life, we can spiritually grow and gather more and more steadiness of mind, called *purity of the inner equipment*. Without a steady mind, spiritual exploration is impossible. "The earlier prescribed friendliness, kindness, etc.,

---

[2] From *Yoga Sūtra Bhāṣya*.

are the values of right relationships; when practiced for a sufficiently long time, they will lead the intelligent seeker to discover a
more steady mind in the contemplation seat."[3]

When the seeker has eliminated all clinging attachments to,
and thirst for, the world, he will find that his concentration propor-
tionately increases. In a purified mind the power of concentration
becomes more dynamic and highly creative. In such a person,
concentration—as applied in his meditation—cannot waver, as he
has conquered all his eagerness to possess and enjoy the objects of
pleasure. When this anxious urge to seek joy in objects has dried up
in him, how can any thoughts arise to drive the seeker into idle
mental wanderings during deep meditation?

The master declares:

Thoughts, turned extrovert and functioning in the
objects are, together and in their entirety, called *citta*. All
meditation is our sincere effort to capture and destroy
the *citta*—"the outward-running thoughts." When the
mind is not engaged in any object, how can thoughts
manifest themselves on the empty horizon of the mind?[4]

Students of meditation, not knowing the mode of their mental
functioning, unnecessarily struggle to quiet their minds and feel
utterly disappointed and discouraged because they are thereby
unwittingly exciting their minds and feeding their thought-agitations.

The engine of the mind functions on the oil of perception. The
mind, running out through the sense organs, reaches the object, and
there it molds itself into the shape of the object; when that "object-
thought" glows in the light of Consciousness in us, the "knowledge
of that object" is born. This is perception, according to Vedanta.
The more the perceptions, the more the agitations. Therefore,
"Perceptions supply the grit for the mill of the mind," say the wise.[5]

---

[3] From *Yoga Sūtra Bhāṣya*.
[4] From *Yoga Vāsiṣṭha*, a text of 6,000 verses in which the sage Vasishtha
gives spiritual instruction to Rama, one of the most popular divine
incarnations in Hinduism.
[5] *Yoga Vāsiṣṭha*.

The rising of the pictures of outer objects and of memories of past experiences in the mind constitutes perception—and so long as these perceptions are rising, the mind will be buzzing with its irresistible activities.

Not to cooperate with the mental dancings and not to lend them the grace of life by our identification with them bring about the exhaustion of *vāsanās*. The end of the *vāsanās* is the annihilation of the mind; and where the mind ends, spiritual ignorance ceases to express itself.

To summarize:

a. To conquer the mind we must reduce our clinging attachments and end our thirst to enjoy objects.

b. When we are eager to master our mind, fewer thoughts arise in us.

c. Perception of objects feeds the engine of our mind and cuts off the steady supply of vitality to the mind.

When thus stripped of its features one by one, the mind dries up and withers away. The mind disappears into the vision of the great, grand fulfillment divine. Hasten thither slowly.

The Subjective
Conquest 29

If we refuse to feed the mind with perceptions of objects, the mind will slowly grind to a stop. Some rishis go still further and declare that the meditator *should give up even the attitude* that he or she is an imagining-thinking entity. It is the mind's function to think, to feel, or to imagine; but these feelings and thoughts cannot arise, and they cannot be maintained by themselves, without an intimate reference to the thinker-feeler ego.

When this idea "I am the thinker-feeler" is renounced by the meditator, he or she becomes an interested observer of the flood of thoughts rising, and soon the very gurgling springs of thought dry up. In due course, the mind ends. In this egoless attitude of detachment the mind becomes extremely subtle and gathers to itself a greater power of penetration to reach deeper meditation.

The mind determines the quality and beauty, the dynamism and glory, the nature and arrangements of the world around us. An extension of our mind in its constant perceptions and interpretations unveils for us our private world of sorrows and joys, likes and dislikes, successes and failures. By conquering the mind we conquer our world. The outer circumstances and the available objects and beings around us can no longer make us dance to their will and whim. We come to call the tune, and the world around us learns to obey as we will it to act.

In fact, without this subjective conquest of our own mind, no conquest anywhere is a real conquest. Even if we have won the whole world, of what avail is it to us if we have not won over the mind? No success is a success, no joy a real joy, no beauty a true beauty unless we have conquered our mind.

Even though you have not conquered, in battles, the
world, you become the world-conqueror when you have

conquered your mind; and although you have for long conquered the world by force, you have conquered nothing of the world so long as you have not conquered yourself.[1]

In order to conquer the mind, we need not run away physically from all sense objects or living beings in our life. All that we have to do is to attend consistently to the taming of the mind. Objects are helpless against a mind under control of the clear intellect. The sense organs will not dare run out into the cesspools of sensuous gratification when the mind behind them is a fully disciplined and strictly cultivated one.

Therefore, instead of unnecessarily wasting our energies in regulating the world of objects and environments, instead of exhausting ourselves in vain attempts at controlling the sense organs, let us attend to the mastering of our mind. The masters say: "Extrovert thought is the commander of the sense organs, and so to win him is to win all; not to win him is to win none . . . just as to one who is wearing shoes the whole world is covered with leather."[2]

You need not conquer the sense organs one by one, nor do you need to run away from all objects of sense fascination. Control the mind—and then go wherever you will. With shoes you can walk even over thorny bushes and stony slopes. You are protected from them all. Conquer your mind, then you are insured against everything, everywhere, at all times.

As a meditator you must thus direct your attention constantly to capturing the wild mind and taming it to obey your own pure decisions and *sāttvic* commands. Once the mind is conquered, all else is conquered. A conquered mind is called *pure mind* in Vedanta. It is mental equipment that is not agitated by every passing mood of passion, nor disturbed by every fascinating object that comes across it.

A pure mind has fewer agitations than an impure one, although some agitations still do exist in it. By following ethical and moral codes of conduct, by cultivating devotion to the Lord, by worship and prayer, by penance and surrender, through study and reflection, by dispassion and meditation upon the Self, we strive to

---

[1] From *Yoga Vāsiṣṭha*.
[2] From *Yoga Vāsiṣṭha*.

bring our mind into a quiet and total silence; and the quieter the mind gets, the more thoroughly conquered the mind becomes.

When the direction of our thoughts is toward the objects of the world, the agitations in the mind increase in number. So long as the thoughts are riotous, we cannot have any mental quietude, and, naturally, we enjoy little success in meditation. Therefore it becomes clear that to quiet the mind it must be switched off from its blind, passionate run after sense objects. Left to itself, the mind in its irresistible energy will run toward its own familiar fields of pleasure. Thereafter it becomes habituated only to move in that limited field of gratification. Once this extrovertedness has become a firm habit with the mind, to persuade it away from its self-destructive preoccupations becomes a painful and herculean task.

The nature of the mind is that its thoughts will readily flow toward any object of love. Where our love is, there our mind goes and lingers. This being its natural and instinctive mode of behavior, if we can supply it with an alternative field of joyous love, it is sure to turn toward it and, in so doing, will turn away from the world of objects, where it is now getting totally dissipated of all its rich potentialities.

This creative altar provided for the mind to hold onto, removed from the storms of worldly temptation, is called the *point of contemplation*. When we thus worship, adore, and meditate upon the chosen Lord of our heart, we give the mind a refreshing altar of contemplation. The altar provides a dry dock for the mind, a safe place away from the stormy confusions of sense enchantments, a place where we may repair and revitalize it.

Devotion (*bhakti*) contributes greatly to the quietude of the mind, which is the beginning of the path of meditation. Rush to it. But haste makes waste; yet, remember to hasten slowly.

The Present Moment

30

When the mind drops its perceptions of sense objects and stops identification with its thought dances, at that stage in meditation, the mind is *no-mind*. When thoughts rush out in their mad fury to hug objects of pleasure, they are called *extrovert thoughts*, and to quiet these is the sacred function of the path of meditation. When these outgoing thoughts are eliminated, the resulting condition of the mind is known as the *no-thought state* of highest meditation.

Thoughts gush in to flood the mind with angry bursts of self-ruinous compulsions mainly from two sources: the past and the future. Some thoughts stem from the past, dragging along with them the memories of the good and bad done in the days gone by. These confuse the individual with the regrets and sorrows, joys and pleasures raised by his memory from the stinking tombs of the past, forcing him to relive the dead past in the fragrant moments of the present. The future is the other source of our thoughts. We are often flown upon the wings of our mind's fancy and imagination to a world of dreams—where we are made to shudder at the future possibilities of failure, tremble in hopes of successes, and swoon in the expectation of total losses or large profits.

The past is made up of dead moments, and to unearth the buried moments is to live with the dead. We do so when we waste our energies in unproductive and wasteful regrets over things we have already committed. The more we remember them, those very *vāsanās* are getting more deeply fixed into our personality structure.

When we are not engaging ourselves with the negative preoccupation of entertaining the regrets of the past, we are wandering in the fairy-castles of our fancied future, peopled with ugly fears, horrid dreams, unnerving hopes, and, perhaps, a thousand impossible expectations.

143

In short, when our minds are not rattled by the perception of objects, let us not thereby conclude that we have quieted our thoughts. Often, it is not so. The mind, when it is not engaged in the worldly objects that are right in front of it, can choose its own private fields of agitation by dragging up the buried corpses of a diseased past or by bringing up vivid pictures of a tragic hopelessness as the sure possibility of the immediate future! In either case the mind of the individual at meditation can get sadly disturbed. Therefore, the rishis advise us: "Moment to moment engage the outgoing mind to live in the present. Completely reject the past. Renounce the future totally. Then, in such a bosom, the agitated mind shall reach the state of mindlessness."[1] This state of mind is called *no-mind.*

The content of the present moment, divorced from all relationships with the past and future, is the absolute fullness of the Infinite. Eternity is experienced at the sacred depth of the present moment. To live in the present, independent of the past and the future, is to experience *samādhi*, the revealing culmination of meditation. Seek it yourself. Nobody can give it to anyone else. Each will have to reach there all by himself, in himself, with no other vehicle than himself.

The sum total of the memories that we retain of our experiences in the past gives us a false notion of ourselves as an "individual entity." This is the personality of our ego. It is this ego—a mere bundle of memories of dead moments—that is meeting the present and interpreting it constantly in terms of its diseased past. Never can the ego see the present *truly as it is.*

Again, when the past, the ego, meets the present, it always strives to weave out of the present a future pattern, a web spun by the ego out of its own imaginations. Hence life is a confusing jumble of meaningless sorrows, purposeless tensions, unproductive strains, depthless joys—all together a mad roar of an inconsistent destiny, dashing against the unyielding actualities of life. In the face of this frothy confusion the individual feels helpless, a mere raft dancing to the whim of the surge around him.

Not to identify yourself with the rising tides of thought but to remain as a witness of them all is a definite stage in the efforts at meditation. In an atmosphere of your own unconcernedness, your

---

[1] From *Yoga Vāsiṣṭha.*

thoughts will get suffocated and will die by themselves. So the rishis advise the seekers on the path of meditation: "Moment to moment disassociate yourself from continuing any thought that consciously rises in the mind. This practice sweeps the mind clean of all rising thoughts, leads you to the state of thoughtlessness, and you arrive at the Holy of holies."[2]

This nonassociation with the rising thought-disturbances is achieved by training ourselves to remain as a witness to the flood of happenings in ourselves. To be a mere onlooker of the lusty parade of thoughts in revelry is to withdraw from thoughts their ability to continue their inner carnival any longer. As a witness we remain in the present, without being conditioned by past associations or enchanted by future expectations. This state, called the *neutral condition of personality*, will, in its sweep and depth, ultimately bring us to the thoughtless condition. This no-mind state is the very divine Substratum upon which the present exists and which serves as the threshold of time where the future becomes the past.

The no-mind state is the experience of pure Awareness, with no distracting objects—only the infinite Self, the Changeless and the Unique. This is the goal to be reached, the Truth to be realized, the experience divine to be lived as the meditator's own essential Self. It is not a thing to be objectively recognized or even intellectually comprehended. This state is to be spiritually apprehended—in an immediate, personal, inner experience. In this state meditation gets fulfilled, and the meditator becomes the one Self, where the triple factors, meditator-meditated-meditation, coalesce to become one vital experience of total transcendental awakening, or Self-realization.

The goal is, no doubt, extremely covetable and supremely enchanting. But to attain it the meditator must have the necessary equipment fully prepared. In our times we find that failures in meditation are reported more often than successes. This is because the seekers, in the spirit of our hurried times, dash into the act of meditation without first procuring the required preflight attunement of their "machines-of-flight." The takeoff never happens!

For establishing a scheme of life most conducive to helping meditators grow into meditative attunement, the masters give

---

[2] From *Yoga Vāsiṣṭha*.

advice in the most general terms: "Stop remembering and craving for things bygone; entertain no joy or sorrow as they reach you in the present; remaining thus, you shall grow into the greater glory of your own Self."[3] Therefore, let us learn to surrender our past unto His feet in love, and let us learn to remain in those sublime heights of divine awareness, where worries and joys cannot reach to cloud our vision and upset our equipoise.

Be patient. Be steady. Strive continuously, cultivating these qualities. Success is sure, and the Upanishad rishis assure for us the experience of the Self. Toward this acme of life hurry without haste; hasten slowly.

---

[3] From *Yoga Vāsiṣṭha*.

The Other Shore
of Saṁsāra

31

The glory of the Vedantic scriptures is that they not only declare the Truth and point out the goal, but they also clearly prescribe ways and means to achieve that goal. This technical know-how available in the Upanishads makes them the most practical and useful texts on Self-perfection available for us. The know-how, however, lies scattered throughout the texts.

When we meditate upon that which is entertaining and pleasant to us, our mind, in its gathering joy and satisfaction, quiets itself and the outgoing thoughts become steadily rooted in contemplation. Thus, the poets in their poetic moods, scientists in their laboratory, artisans at their work—all of them discover a joy that is not typical of what we usually experience in the mind. This joy arises subjectively from the steadiness of the mind.

However steady the mind may become—and even get filled with the noblest of thoughts—the mind still exists, and so long as the mind survives, thought-agitations veil the Self under a mist of mind-created confusions raised in thoughts. This mind is the cause for the nonapprehension of the real essence in us, which is our own being, the eternal Self. Hence, the mind is to be completely sublimated. In the last stages we can say that the mind "disappears into vision"—meaning, when the mind disappears, the vision of the ultimate Reality takes place.

A noted saint-queen, Choodala, advises her despondent royal husband and encourages him to put forth still more efforts at intelligent and effective meditation:

> The mind is the source of all *vāsanās* and so is all. It lies spread in all objects of perception and therefore it is all-pervading. The mind projects all the perceived and

147

experienced world, and so it is the source for all things. When the mind renounces all—when it is gathered from all the variety of things that constitute the world—you have renounced all.[1]

When the mind stands thus in utter nakedness, it is the no-mind. And that is the auspicious moment of illumination.

Thus viewed, the entire call of the rishis is for us to emerge from the limitations of our own mind equipment. Conditioned by the mind, the Self appears to be mortal, finite, limited. The Self clothed in the mind is the ego, jīva.

This ego, thoughtlessly assuming an independent and separate existence for itself, naturally sees the whole world as a mighty, endless array of things and beings, of circumstances and situations—all of them inimical to itself. It feels lonely; in its loneliness it is overwhelmed by fear. To assure its own security, the ego thereafter builds mighty phantom-fortresses around itself with frail wealth, impermanent name, flimsy fame, disloyal relations, and undependable friends, and maintains a thousand treacherous relationships with a million things and beings. But still, the ego feels insecure, frightened, lonely, unhappy, and altogether entirely cheated!

"End the mind and remain great" is the thunderous bidding from every corner of the halls of Vedanta, echoing and reechoing in the ears of all sincere students. "Annihilate the mind and remain great. Reaching the other shore of saṃsāra, become the ever-pure Self. Even after long, long years of contemplation we can still find a trace of the scum called the mind in the pure Self."[2]

To realize that the mind can never be in the infinite Consciousness, the Self, because the Self is ever pure, is the end of the mind. An illusory power superimposed on the Self, by our own delusion, is the mind.

Pause! Think! Quiet the mind!

Experience that which comes to vision on the mind's disappearance. The immediate experience—"That Self am I"—is the realization.

In this subjective experience of our own Self we must be able to rise above all our low identifications with the baser aspects of our

---

[1] From Yoga Vāsiṣṭha.
[2] From Yoga Vāsiṣṭha.

personality. Identifying with our body, we prop up our physical personality and come to demand a life of physical gratifications. Becoming one with the mind, we gather a psychological identity and suffer all the mental disturbances in us. Attuning ourselves to our thoughts, we play the part of the intellectual person, suffering in ourselves all the agitations caused by the restlessness of the intellect. Once we drop these false projections, which we have ourselves manufactured, we resign from the ignoble world of objects-emotions-thoughts, which our body-mind-intellect complex provides for our own suffering.

This process of knowingly distilling away Consciousness from these layers of matter-equipment, in an act of consummate meditation upon the pure Self, the eternal Life-Spark in us, is explained in detail by the ancient rishis in the language of the Vedas. Using the *yajña* ritual (sacrifice-ritual) as a metaphor, the rishi says, "A reflective seeker, by tuning his thoughts to the Self, offers all the three worlds as straws into the fire, and all his delusions get burned up."[3] Through steady meditation upon the Self, the mental projections and consequent experiences of the worlds of waking, dream, and deep sleep get rolled up and burned like dry grass in the fire of Self-realization.

This realization is to be achieved by each one of us, all by ourselves, in ourselves, for ourselves. We need to note modes of living conducive to these attempts at self-evolution, as they constitute the spiritual values. At the highest peak of the divine life stands the mighty temple of meditation. In your climb toward it, hasten slowly.

---

[3] From *Yoga Vāsiṣṭha*.

Study, Japa, and Meditation 32

How are seekers to implement the technique of meditation in their life of day-to-day worldly problems and agitations, imaginations and fantasies, passions and pangs, hopes and despairs?

The path of *sādhanā* must be intelligent, and it must be within the abilities of an average person to practice—if not always with ready ease and quick results, at least, when continued sincerely, with a certain amount of heroic effort and some rewarding results. Else in disappointment an average seeker will leave the path and its pursuit.

The Upanishad seers discovered a very attractive and pleasant-looking path to help us get established on the road to Reality. They seem to point out a steadily rising bridle path up to the higher summits of the mystic peaks. Thereafter, each may find his or her way clearly to the crown. Study of the scriptures, in a spirit of total participation—augmented with frequent listening to the learned exponents and a few direct contacts with the authoritative masters—is found to be very helpful in the beginning. This regular study of the Upanishads, the *Gītā*, and other spiritual literature[1] is called *svādhyāya.*

With or without the help of a *mālā* or mantra, continuously fixing our mind on the divine imports and spiritual suggestions of the mystic word thus repeated is called *japa.* This technique keeps the mind always uplifted, away from the dark world of objects and their distracting fascinations, and pointed toward the reviving

---

[1] *Rāmāyaṇa, Bhāgavatam, Yoga Vāsiṣṭha, Sukh-Mani, Guru Granth Sahib, Ātmā Bodha, Vivekacūḍāmaṇi,* and *Bhaja Govindam* can also be adopted as texts for serious and deep study.

climes of the final spiritual illumination. Thoughts become less violent, and the mind becomes more and more introvert.

When the thoughts have thus been nourished by study (*svādhyāya*) and rendered quiet and peaceful by *japa*, to rest the hushed mind at the altar of the Self in a thrilled mood of choiceless contemplation is meditation (*dhyāna*).

The rishis encourage us to combine judiciously these three main paths of study, *japa*, and meditation, and thus deny the mind the least chance to wander freely into the spiritually unhygienic fields of sense gratification. A great master advises us:

> After listening, study, and *japa*, practice meditation.
> After emerging from meditation, engage in listening,
> study, and *japa*. After *japa*, meditate again. At the end
> of meditation, pursue *japa*. One who is thus well
> trained in *japa* and meditation is a steady seeker upon
> whom the supreme Auspiciousness is sure to shower
> His grace.[2]

While listening we only *participate* in spiritual life. When we study we get *involved* in the ideas to which we listened. In *japa* our involvement deepens, and in meditation we get ourselves totally *committed* to the ideal, which is the goal of all spiritual seekers.

The agitations of the mind-and-intellect equipment create an impenetrable thought-barrier between our sense of ego and our divine status as infinite Consciousness, which we are in our essential nature. All spiritual practices are training by which the disturbances of the thoughts in our mind are brought to a minimum.

When a meditator's mind has thus become hushed into a relatively quiet attitude, his meditation gathers an extra flight and efficiency. His mind is filled with the cool content of peace, and an unearthly joy spreads and dances in his heart. This state of expansion within, which invokes an unusual quality of inner joy and thrill, leaving behind for some time a subjective sense of holiness and contentment, is the first experience that assures the student of a richer reward awaiting him at the end of his journey. Once the student experiences this joy, he will never more become irregular in his meditation. All other external obstructions get rejected and

---

[2] From *Yoga Vāsiṣṭha*.

ignored. Nothing can any longer entice the seeker away from his regular meditation sessions.

He begins to regulate, reorganize, and readjust his daily programs. Activities, objects of interest, contacts, engagements, duties, and even his professional responsibilities—all undergo a salutary reorientation. Until now his activities and relationships had been based upon his maximum physical comfort and sense gratification. Now his life becomes oriented for meditation.

He lives a pure life of dedication, truthfulness, and deep devotion. He engages himself only in peaceful, God-centered activities. All the promises of joys, which he had pursued so long, can no longer carry any attraction for him. He retires from all such contacts that might bring even the slightest mental fatigue or disturbance, for a fatigued mind cannot reach and maintain high altitudes of meditation. And without the mystic vitality, poise in meditation will be totally absent.

The more a seeker's mind retires from its direct involvement in the world of sense objects and from attachment to things and beings, the more he develops what Vedanta technically calls *retirement*. As the mind retires from the world outside, it enters more and more into the subtler realms of the Essence. Those subtler realms are the mystic regions of strange beauty, of unearthly brilliance, of heavenly melody, of supersensuous joys. Retirement of the mind leads it to extreme peace.

The masters of meditation have no hesitation in openly and distinctly declaring that retirement is extreme peace, and those who practice it shall experience that their spiritual unfoldment is directly proportional to their success in retirement from mental engagements with the outer world.[3] To the extent the seeker clutches himself off from worldly lust-prompted activities, to that extent his becomes the march toward the culminating goal of meditation: the total quietude of the mind, the still intellect, the transcendental experience—called *samādhi*.

No progress in any walk of life is possible without leaving the present state and moving forward to win the new state of greater glory. No growth is possible unless we are willing to drop out of our previous condition and accept the ampler status of the new

---

[3] *Śaṅkara Bhāṣya.*

condition. Childhood must end in the youngster; youth must end in the grown man. If a bud is not ready to end its present state, how can it grow and unfold itself to become a flower?

Our mental power, so entirely invested today in our outward life, must be turned, in all its rich strength, to the life within. Naturally, to the extent to which we are successful in curbing the lower mind from its play in the lower planes, to that extent the higher mind shall discover itself reveling in its own meditative flights in the higher planes of Consciousness.

Remember always to hasten sincerely, but slowly.

Inner Repose 33

The topic of our discussion has been: how to practice the science of Reality (*brahmavidyā*). This great science has been indicated by the spiritual masters in different ways:

> Through the elimination of all perceptions, when our mind is uplifted from its natural oscillations between its likes and dislikes, we experience a subjective thrill of joy. To strive to reach this state of experience is called *practicing the science of Reality.* [1]

Thus, the authoritative definition of spiritual practice itself gives us a clear hint that it embraces two main schemes: (a) a scheme to withdraw our anxious awareness of the sense objects, perceived through our sense organs, and (b) yet another scheme to control the very attitude of our mind during these sense contacts. A mind full of likes and dislikes must always get irresistibly flooded with sense perceptions. The direction of its devastating march and the extent of destruction it would thereafter perpetrate are determined by the springs of its birth—whether it got flooded due to its likes or due to its dislikes.

It is thus clear that a seeker who is after her own spiritual rehabilitation must, first of all, strive to tame her sense organs and calm her mind, cultivating the more enduring values of life through such practices as study, *japa*, meditation, the company of the good, prayers, and selfless service to others. Once the mind goes wild, all good resolves are of no avail, and the sense organs are helplessly whipped up and forced into the hunt for sense objects.

---

[1] From *Yoga Vāsiṣṭha*.

Even when our mind is quiet, if our sense organs are not fully tamed, they can flood the calm mind with a deluge of fascinating thoughts of sense pleasure. Naturally, we must learn to keep under check both the outer and inner teams of instruments. When the two above-indicated schemes are successfully fulfilled, the victory is followed by an enthralling feeling of satisfaction. The heart of the seeker gets filled with a sense of complete satisfaction at the very richness of the life it has come to live. This sense of fullness is totally subjective—it has nothing to do with the presence of a conducive environment.

In such a calm person of inner repose, the sense organs are easily tamed. The seers tell us: "When the seeker leaves all the likes and dislikes of the mind and refills himself with contemplations upon the nature of the Self, all the organs of perception-feeling-thinking become extremely quiet."[2]

In our present way of life, we blindly run along the existing currents of thought in the mind; they are all extrovert, driven out by the mind for its desire fulfillment. In this furious, mad rush, the specific objects toward which our thoughts gush at any given moment are determined by the mind's likes and dislikes. In short, the behavior of the mind is determined by what the mind's passing fancy of the moment happens to be.

To quiet the mind, the seeker practices steady contemplation upon the nature of the Self, which he has heard about, reflected upon, and, in his own reasoning, got fully convinced about. By so employing the mind, the seeker curbs or halts its rush toward objects and redirects it toward the immutable Light within, the Self. Naturally, the mind comes to rest; and when the mind rests, the sense organs become entirely vanquished and enslaved.

The force with which the sense organs run, and the depth to which they can drag us down in our worldly life, will depend upon the frequency of agitations in our mind; and these agitations depend upon the type of values or motives we entertain. The quality of the values we respect gets reflected in the quality of thoughts we entertain, and the nature of our thoughts determines the texture and nobility of our actions.

When the values are low, utterly selfish, and extremely ego-centered (*tāmasic*), the thoughts are dull, gross, and even animalistic, and naturally actions arising out of them can only be

---

[2] From *Yoga Vāsiṣṭha.*

unintelligent, undignified, and meant solely for the gratification of baser passions.

When the motives are slightly nobler, but centered around a person's own selfish ego, with a tendency to be extremely passionate and supremely ambitious (*rājasic*), then they will produce a rougher frequency in his thought-movements. Actions being faithful expressions of inherent thought-patterns, the activities of such *rājasic* persons can only be dynamic, as they seek gratification of their own selfish desires and personal ambitions.

The noblest (*sāttvic*) motives alone can bring the mind into a state of alert attention to catch the passing tunes of the eternal rhythm all around and within. The thoughts of such people have a noiseless charm, and their activities have a compelling grace, an enchanting beauty, a pleasing aura, and a self-evident glow of holiness.

When the mind is in the *tāmasic* condition, it has to be whipped up with a dash of desire into the *rājasic* type. The *rājasic* mind must learn to continue and even step up the dynamism of action, but give up more and more of its selfish attitudes. This selfless attitude lifts the mind up into the peace and inner joy of the *sāttvic* type; and with such a change in the texture of the mind, the personality of the individual also changes. Such *sāttvic* individuals are marked for great success in meditation, and in a short time. Seekers should therefore strive to cultivate this graceful attitude of *sattva* by training themselves to live a life of discrimination (*viveka*) and dispassion (*vairāgya*), of study and reflection, of prayer and discussion, of contemplation and meditation.

All *sāttvic* students are sure to succeed spectacularly when they subject themselves to spiritual practice seriously and sincerely. May success attend all. Hasten slowly, please.

Transforming Influences

34

The nature of the mind alone determines the type of persons we are. In fact, as our *vāsanās*—our urges and motives, the subsurface motivating factors within our emotional profile—so are our thoughts; and as our thoughts, so are our actions. Usually, a person is assessed solely by his actions. The intelligent critics will evaluate a person by his feelings. A rare few intelligent ones alone can truly judge a person and his character through correct insight into his thoughts and motives.

In fact, "as we think, so we become" is a relevant and valid statement declared by the closest students of human behavior. The attempts of a meditator are to revolutionize the structure and function of his mind. This is the inner content of all effective schemes for taming the mind.

The thoughts with which we ardently feed our conscious mind slowly seep through its various layers to influence its subtler subconscious layers. A person is constantly influenced by his physical surroundings, consisting of objects, and by his mental environment, provided by the type of ideas suggested to his mind. We are generally unconscious of this inescapable field of influences that always surround us.

Naturally, the rude, the vulgar, the sensuous, the lusty, the selfish, the immoral, the crude—all are mentally breathed in during our day's transactions. Only the rare few minds of alert seekers or strong personalities have something like a safety mechanism at work to resist—if not actually to reject—these baser contagions.

To a student of meditation, therefore, the teacher lovingly points out and tenderly insists upon the need for frequent retreats, daily contacts with inspiring people, and daily study of the scriptures in order to gather a refreshingly rejuvenating feed of ideas with which to nourish the mind. These are the essential items of practice in the day-to-day life of a sincere aspirant to meditation.

When the conscious outer surface of the mind is made to play in the company of such ideas, in holy surroundings, their transforming influence slowly drips down to water the lower layers of the subconscious and finally percolates further to enthrall even the unconscious levels of the mind. This is seen in our daily life. Says a rishi:

> As a wise man intensively lives a life of study and good
> companionship with other wise men in his waking
> hours, so too will his dream world be full of discussions
> with wise men. Whatever the mind takes up with
> intense ardor determines the type of experience invoked
> by that mind in its life outside.[1]

Hence we have the wise saying: "Mind is the man." Shankara, in a thunderous assertion, says:

> For all creatures, mind alone is the cause for "bondage"
> and "freedom"! Mind muddied with agitations (rajas)
> binds man to his passions with attachments, while the
> same mind, free from passions (sattva), is the instrument
> to free man from all his inhibitions and perversions, and
> to take him to the eternal abode of his essential
> Selfhood.[2]

When a mind is thus trained to withdraw from its present fields of ruinous dissipations and gets recharged with its freshly opened springs of dynamism through regular and steady contemplation, the lower mind ascends to be the higher and nobler mind. As the purification increases, the mind scales higher and higher, until at last the purest mind becomes no-mind, which reveals the Self, the Reality. The mind ends in a blaze of illumination.

The more a seeker unnecessarily and unintelligently worries over his mind and its caprices, the more the mind grows in grossness and asserts itself upon the seeker's inner world. Ignore the

---

[1] From *Yoga Vāsiṣṭha.*

[2] From *Vivekacūḍāmaṇi* by Shankara.

mind. Overlook its prattlings and vagaries. Conquer it with under-standing. Never create a stalemate in your confrontation with the mind. Where you cannot at this moment directly meet the mind and win it over, ignore it in that field and attack it where it is weak. Observe and understand its weaknesses and its usual strategies. Outwit it by diplomatic moves, by assertion of your essential lordship over it. Now and then allow the mind to beat you down and smile away the defeat with a sportsman's spirit of fairness and ease. Be cheerful. Feel confident in the Lord's grace and in the ultimate victory.

This battle is an inner guerrilla war. The enemy is never out in the open. He ducks and hides, comes out, thrusts, devastates, and runs to hide again. We have to counter all his unexpected moves, surprise him in his hideouts, and catch him in his acts. Alertness and vigilance alone can promise the final victory.

In this battle, remember to use the irresistible, mighty weapon of true Knowledge of the Self. In the final analysis, the mind is nothing but an inert matter layer, subtle and therefore apparently more powerful than the sense organs. Yet, it is only matter, and matter is ever inert. The mind draws its strength from the Self and then proceeds to veil Its blissful domain. To those who doubt whether this is possible, the masters indicate how darkness born out of a cave veils the cave and gives us fears of ghosts and the like. Similarly, the mind born of the Self veils the Self, and instead of Its pure bliss and peace, we get only the ego-experience of cancerous pains and blistering passions.

Shankara's pen deftly paints an example from nature: "Just as clouds born of the sun's rays cover the sun, so the mind and ego, born of the Self, veil the Self and play as though there were no Self behind them."[3]

Mind is nothing but the Self, and the Consciousness of the Self is the power from which the mind draws its strength to act and function. A seeker must assume intelligently a get-tough stance with the mind. It is a *negative* approach to deny the mind its full and uncurbed freedom to do and to act as it wills. This denial is to be steadily supplemented with a *positive* program of refusing to co-operate with the mind and of standing as a quiet witness of the mind's demands and its devil-dances, its maddening rush into

---

[3] From *Vivekacūḍāmaṇi.*

objects of pleasure, its clinging attachment to beings, its joys and sorrows, fears and pains, loves and lusts, pride and passions. This alert witness stands on the balcony of the intellect and watches the self-exhausting excesses of the mind.

When a meditator stands thus as a witness of his own mind, he will notice how the tempo of his mind's drunken revelry slowly quiets down. And, in time, if he succeeds in not getting himself involved in his mind's death-dance, he will see how it comes to a spent-out halt. When we don't lend our interest to the pursuit of sense pleasures, the mind cannot continuously engage, by itself, in its hunt for objects of sense gratification. We ourselves loan out the dynamism to the inert mind, and the mind, so fattened by our own cooperation, threatens our inner peace.

Withdraw your grace from the mind. The mind is the devil who has invoked you and received your own blessings, and it is now threatening to annihilate you! Learn to destroy him quickly—but hasten slowly.

Evolutionary
Unfoldment

35

The mind threatens our inner peace with the very strength we unwittingly lend to it. In itself the mind is inert. It has no life of its own. It is dead matter, ever inert and insentient. Without fuel, an automobile cannot dash forth. By itself, it is just a mass of heavy iron shaped as the engine! Iron by itself has no locomotion. When the driver steps on the gas, the heavy engine harnesses all its horsepower and dashes forth, pantingly eating up great distances. It can stop only when the driver takes his foot off the gas; then, by itself, the vehicle slows down to reach a complete halt—if the driver remains as a careful witness of the switched-off car exhausting its gathered momentum. In the same way, the mind will come to a halt if the meditator withdraws his enthusiastic participation in the mind's lusty excesses.

In fact, the rishis who mastered their minds and conquered the peaks of Self-realization look back laughingly at their own past and anxiously at our frantic efforts to tame our minds. They are staggered. Wonder chokes them. Surprise smothers them. Breathless in their amazement, they burst out: "Mind is an inert thing. It cannot exist by itself. Therefore, we can say that it is a dead thing (inert). And this world dies and decays because of this dead thing called the mind—what a strange wheel of stupidity!"[1]

To experience such a realization is to get away, in a trice, from the apparent might and power of the mind. To yield yourself constantly to the delusory strength of the mind and to lose your confidence in yourself is to surrender to the dream-phantom called the mind. Cultivate faith in yourself, in the path you are following,

---

[1] From *Yoga Vāsiṣṭha*.

and in the ultimate goal. Your faith should not result from seduction by the scriptures of a hoary age or from your awe-inspired adoration of your teacher. Faith built upon knowledge, reflection, and practice alone can be truly fruitful.

Also, let us understand that to "possess" faith is a sheer, futile mental shackle. The faith in a truth which we now possess may leave us at any moment, all of a sudden, plunging us into utter darkness. Let the faith in us grow to possess us. We do not want to possess a faith; we require a faith that will possess us! Such a faith-possessed seeker's attempts at meditation can alone be valid efforts in the spiritual field. Win your victory through right efforts.

The way of gaining this inner victory over the mind has been sung by the masters:

> All tragedies and sorrows in life come by false and
> wrong willing. By right willing the mind helps the
> seekers to gain the higher states in Heaven. Holding the
> mind in joy, and so in quietude, stop all willing and thus
> win the final victory over the mind.[2]

The sum total of the willing-power is that which maintains the individual concept of a separate entity, the ego. It is this ego in us that is suffering all the limitations of life. Such a miserable life of endless sorrows alone is possible in an ego-oriented arrangement of things. The attempt of an intelligent meditator is to *revolutionize* the world, now running under an ego-oriented order of power and pleasure, through an *evolutionary* unfoldment within, into a God-oriented system of peace and perfection. Today all our energies are spent, every moment, in catering to the whims and fancies of this ego, the I, in us. To reestablish the Selfhood within by ending this lower ego is the cherished goal of all seekers of higher meditation.

A noble master has exhaustively laid down the means for ending this tyrannical ego and its unchallenged cruel rule. He consoles us as he declares:

> One who has renounced all vanity, permanently living
> in self-control and reflecting upon the noble glory of the
> Self, must serve "the good." All these worldly objects

---

[2] From *Yoga Vāsiṣṭha*.

and their glories are a magic of the deluded mind. "I
have no occasion to have love for these things, nor need
I detach myself from these nonexistent illusions"— if
you thus maintain a continuous awareness within
yourself, the ego will never more rise up in your bosom.[3]

It now becomes clear that we can ultimately get rid of our ego
only when we have lived our life intelligently. No one can escape
life. Every happening, every experience is a necessary step toward
the great, grand goal. Life supplies experiences, but we never make
full use of them. The ego is but a bundle consisting of the dead
moments and their memories from our past life. In fact, we always
carry a corpse on our shoulders! Embracing this decaying filth, we
can never enter the holy sanctum of Truth. Hence vanity, born of
false identification with body-mind-intellect, must be given up.

This sacrifice is not possible unless we practice self-control in
the outward flight of our thoughts toward the pleasures of sense
objects. And this cannot happen without diverting the mind to
contemplate upon the glory and holiness of the divine Self. To keep
the mind elevated with a sense of holiness within, we must constantly practice "service of the good," meaning of saints and sages,
in the form of devoted study and deep reflection upon the sacred
scriptures given out by these noble souls. Their companionship
gives the necessary lift for the mind to maintain its height and
balance.

When a seeker has thus purified himself by the above processes and remains continuously in the awareness of the illusory
nature of the objects of sense enchantments, he has no chance of
experiencing the play of the ego. The ego is merely the entity that
is raised by the "doer-enjoyer-am-I" attitude. Our sense of doership
and enjoyership creates and sustains, nurtures and nourishes our
ego.

Thus, a pair of verses reveals the entire scheme for hunting
down the ego. Seekers who jump into their meditation seats without preparing themselves for the "flight" crash even at the very
"takeoff." Time spent in the necessary adjustments of relationships
in the outer world and in the tuning up of the inner equipment is not
time wasted.

---

[3] From *Yoga Vāsiṣṭha.*

When the ego disappears, the vision of the Reality comes. A wise saint used an unforgettable idiom when he said that at the culmination of meditation the ego of the meditator "disappears into the vision of the Infinite."[4]

Your goal is to make your identity with the ego disappear into the vision of the eternal Self. Be—just BE. This will move you to ecstasy, by giving you a gleam of the spirit that shines through the heart of all things. It will be but a cloudy vision at first, and the early visions will disappear, each in resplendent, quick succession. Let them go and then reappear. Each glimpse revives, rejuvenates, resurrects. Thereafter, the meditator's personality totally changes, and, in the end, it comes to shine with an unearthly poise and serenity.

Use no force. Let spirituality open you up into fulfillment, as a bud opens itself into a flower. Hasten slowly.

---

[4] Sri Aurobindo.

Consistent Efforts 36

It is a fact that very many are disappointed in their spiritual attempts, and they find themselves often worse off than they were before, even after years of daily meditation. Such sad failures are primarily due to the seekers' unpreparedness to merit an entry into the higher realms of Consciousness.

Again, even after full preparedness, some may find themselves stagnated for long periods, without moving ahead and reaching the promised fullness in spirituality. Such stagnation is essentially a sign that the meditator is getting entangled with his own subtle attachments with the outer world of objects and with his own inner world of emotions and thoughts. When the mind is loaded down with its own inhibitions, it cannot enter into the subtle layers of the higher Consciousness. The mind must first become fully detached from its delusory preoccupations with its worldly inhibitions; else it will not be able to move from the sheltering base to the serene peaks.

One must constantly strive to detach one's mind from all its play, performed in its false and exhausting identification with the matter vestures. He who constantly seeks to withdraw the mind from its functioning in the "not-Self" by lifting his thoughts to the contemplation of the Self is called a true striver. The masters declare, "Annihilation of the mind comes readily to one who is not excited easily and who is a steady striver."[1]

Even when a meditator has successfully detached his mind from almost all objects and is steadily striving to lift it into steady contemplation, often we find that he, who was progressively proceeding on his path, suddenly becomes dispirited, dejected, and

---

[1] From *Jīvanmukti Viveka* by Shankara.

even diabolically belligerent with the spiritual path. He experiences a slip—and a painful fall. Thereafter, very few have been found to have the guts to get up and walk the path again, all by themselves. To realize, through one's own self-criticism, what were the causes in oneself for the experienced fall is to rediscover the required energy to get up and start moving on the path again.

We must discover the enthusiasm in ourselves to pour out consistent efforts in pursuing the pilgrimage and reaching the temple of Truth. Faith, born of knowledge, supplies the enthusiasm that generates steady reflection and concentration in all thought-applications. This enthusiasm can come only when we get involved in our studies, participate in our reflections, and come to feel totally committed to the path of meditation.

Says Shankara: "There are some who will fail to catch the theme; there are others who will forget what has been told to them clearly. Long periods of repeated contact and discussions with the saints and sages are recommended for both types."[2]

And one who is thus sincerely putting forth the right effort is assured of help from an unknown power, God's unfailing grace. Shankara declares further: "Regardless of the efforts, one who strives to rest his thoughts steadily in the supreme Self, him the Lord blesses."[3]

Continuous and regular practice, done for a long time, can add up in imperceptible accumulation to become a great magazine of power which can, all of a sudden, rocket the mind of the seeker to surprising heights of brilliant meditation. This is the Lord's grace in full manifestation.

When, as a result of our diligent and sincere efforts, we seem to have for once persuaded the restless mind away from all the enticing objects outside, still we cannot say that all the problems are totally solved. The mind is by its very nature very restless; indeed, restlessness of thoughts is the mind. It can build castles-in-the-air and can frisk about in that imagined world among its dreamy fantasies. "On some rare occasions the mind looks apparently disengaged from the objects outside, and the seeker congratulates himself. Yet, the thought-monkey can start again to jump about in a projected world among remembered and fancied objects."[4]

---

[2] From *Jīvanmukti Viveka*.

[3] From *Jīvanmukti Viveka*.

[4] From *Yoga Vāsiṣṭha*.

In short, the conquest of the mind is not easy for the uncontrolled and unheroic seeker. The conquered mind is the reward of continuous efforts, applied with heroism, by one who is supremely sincere, tirelessly persevering, and blessed by right knowledge.

The student of meditation, thus carefully feeling his way upward on his path, may now and then slip and suffer apparent falls here and there for short periods of time. These jerks are very painful and can often blunt the keen edge of the seeker's enthusiasm for spiritual progress. Generally, he attributes it all to a lack of "God's grace" or "guru's blessings." But the naked truth is that the human being is very clever at self-deception, and a seeker is no exception. We deceive ourselves by satisfying some harmless little demands of the flesh, or some mental tickling, or some intellectual fancy. We are very adroit at justifying our own weaknesses and discovering a thousand convincing arguments to excuse ourselves.

Thus, we compromise our ideal by seeking the temporary gratification of some whim of our mind. On such occasions the usual justification is that it is a necessary evil. And it sounds like quite an acceptable excuse in the ears of our society. But a spiritual student must avoid this thorny bush and should never think of taking shelter behind its poisonous foliage. Invariably we find that "a necessary evil" very soon becomes "more and more necessary" and, as we repeat the evil again and again, it becomes "less and less evil" in our own judgment! This is how a compromise once made tends to perpetuate itself as a habit of the mind.

It is through such unconscious cracks that the meditative powers, cultivated and stored up in us, slowly leak out, and our inner life becomes empty of all its acquired beauty and glory.

Be alert. Be vigilant. Avoid all compromises. Be firm on the principles of self-control. Never compromise. Yield not to the mind's charms. Fight them down. Keep cheerful. Turn the mind to the Lord. In devotion cry out for help from the Lord and the teacher. Sing the Lord's glories. Repeat your mantra. Redirect the mind and channel it to reach the thoughts divine. Success is sure for the sincere. Stop not until the goal is reached. But remember to hasten—but slowly.

Inner Silence 37

In the world we can find everywhere people of great intelligence with vast amounts of information and deep erudition. They are to be respected for their industry, study, and powers of memory. They can even be very good sources of inspiration for others. They can excite, encourage, and even cultivate great values of life in others. But unless they have cultivated inner silence, they rot in their own viciousness, excesses, and intemperance.

An open-hearted master is never secretive. He declares, in the most unambiguous language: "One may reflect long upon the words of the scriptures; for long thereafter one may teach others; but without the inner silence arising out of total *vāsanā*-destruction, the supreme State cannot be experienced."[1]

Generally we are apt to take an eloquent or deep-thinking philosopher as an ideal person—but, in fact, he may not be an ideal human being. The mystical experience of the transcendental is a thing apart. To reach that experience requires more than study, or the efforts spent in training, disciplining, and correctly applying the mind. It requires the final rediscovery and, therefore, a first-hand experience of one's own real nature, which is ever divine and most auspicious.

Living constantly in the body-vehicle and identifying with it, we have come to forget our Godly nature to live a fruitless, miserable life of passions and inner agitations. To quiet those agitations and to thrust ourselves above them is spiritual life. To silence the mind and to reach a state wherein we experience an infinite self-expansion is the cherished destination, the rewarding goal. The processes by which we accomplish this goal constitute

---

[1] From *Yoga Vāsiṣṭha*.

our spiritual *sādhanā*, the final reaches of which are gained through meditation.

As a seeker successfully reaches a certain point of self-discipline, his meditation appears to become rewarding. He starts experiencing some strange things—only some of a million varieties of possibility—such as enthralling visions, fascinating sounds, pleasant smells, melting touches, and delicious tastes. He may experience enveloping darkness, expanding rings of effulgence, a flood of blinding light with or without clouds, or melodious music.

When the *gross* world of sense objects is conquered, the mind of the meditator tries to entangle him in such pleasant, heavenly, and enchanting *subtle* sense experiences. These experiences arise from the "subtle elements" and are delusions of the meditator's own mind. They are to be rejected, denied, and destroyed—in fact, according to the rishis, "literally killed and thrown completely away from the bosom."[2] It is said: "Like heroic soldiers who cut down their enemies with their swords, so too the courageous seeker with the sword of his discrimination did cut down the various illusory thought-pictures that rose in him during his meditation."[3] Many such obstacles have to be intelligently met, consistently fought against, and discreetly gotten rid of before an ordinary seeker can reach his goal, the vision of the Self.

Any experiences that we may get are delusory projections of the dying mind. We must reject them all and rise above them. On the peak of purity dwells the infinite Self, the one eternal Substratum for all the illusory world-perceptions and experiences. In order to arrive there and awaken to our own true nature divine, we have to leave all other perceptions and end our participation in the world of plurality. Unless we leave this plane of existence, the Higher cannot be gained. Nothing of "this" can ever be successfully smuggled across the frontiers into "that." The state of Selfhood is unique; it transcends all the experiences of the lower plane. However, from the perspective of the higher state, the realized saint may admit that the transcendental dimension includes the experiences of the limited world also and that the two are not separate.

Consistent practice with firm faith in oneself, constant study, daily reflection, deep devotion, and unbroken awareness of the

---

[2] From *Śaṅkara Bhāṣya*.
[3] From *Śaṅkara Bhāṣya*.

presence of the Lord deep in the personality—these roughly chalk out the path. The person who maintains the spiritual attitude of dedication unto the Supreme and dynamically works in cheerful contentment, ever joyously feeling that he is serving the Lord, is the one who finds his meditation unobstructed. He can smoothly glide into realms of widening expanse of joy and brilliance, peace and perfection.

To be overly conscious of the mind, and in this preoccupation with the mind and its awesome enchantments to lose all faith in ourselves, is to unconsciously keep ourselves under the suzerainty of the mind, almost perpetually. Remember, so long as one is *in* a problem, one can never reach *out* of that problem. The mind is the gruesome problem for a seeker in meditation. So long as he allows himself to be hypnotized by the powers of the mind, he is getting himself more and more identified with the mind—the thought-flow in him—which is but the manifestation of his own nonapprehension of the Self.

Therefore, the masters tell us: "These outgoing thoughts are the products of our mind-identification, which is ignorance. Don't give them a chance to enter your heart. 'I have no outgoing thought'—nonidentification with the mind—is wisdom, and the mind ends."[4]

Stay in the resulting tranquil state of meditation as long as you can; stay undisturbed. Don't disturb that state by initiating new thought-channels. Just remain in it, quietly tuned up to receive, rather than to remember and translate the experience.

Allow meditation to take charge of you. Surrender to His will and grace.

Alert! Quiet! Quietly alert! Alertly quiet!

At your seat of meditation daily strive: haste makes waste, yet hasten slowly.

---

[4] From *Śaṅkara Bhāṣya*.

The Dawn
of Wisdom 38

Recognition of the mind's existence and total identification with it are the play of spiritual ignorance consisting of (a) the nonapprehension of Reality and (b) the consequent misapprehension of It. When we fail to apprehend the wayside post, we misunderstand it to be a ghost, and the ghost-vision gives rise to fear, confusion, and a raised pulse rate! To deny the mind and its outgoing thoughts and to recognize them as flickerings of the Self, the Consciousness, is to annihilate the mind. The end of the mind is the dawn of wisdom (*jñāna*).

Our spiritual teachers with paternal kindness chalk out for us the entire route of our pilgrimage to the Self: "When the sense organs are not engaged in the seeking of and indulging in the sense objects, they remain in their own nature and do not then drag the thoughts into the field of sense gratifications."[1] Again, "When this self-withdrawal from the theaters of sense gratification is practiced, all sense organs come under the will and total control of the seeker."[2] Thereafter, "The meditator—through faith built upon right knowledge (*śraddhā*), self-control (*brahmacarya*), devoted concentration, and intelligent, self-disciplining austerities—cultivates quietude of the mind, which steadily grows in him under these spiritual practices."[3] And, "Devotion for Narayana, worship of Him, and dedication of all activities unto Him ensure for the meditator His grace, and the Lord blesses him soon with the supreme experience of the Self divine."[4]

No one can ever have any chance to complain of difficulties

---

[1] From *Yoga Sūtra Bhāṣya*.
[2] From *Yoga Sūtra Bhāṣya*.
[3] From *Jīvanmukti Viveka*.
[4] From *Yoga Sūtra Bhāṣya*.

en route if he is following this grand road to the goal. Problems arise, progress gets choked, confusions confound, faith departs, despair strangles, and the seeker gets hurled from the path only because of his own inner unpreparedness. Deep-seated urges and inclinations (*vāsanās*) have to be thrown up from the unconscious to the level of the conscious mind. They may play for awhile in us and then will depart, never to return—if we have developed the necessary stamina and discovered sufficient guts to stand apart from them as a disinterested witness during their threatening uprise. Such frequent explosions are unavoidable in any seeker on the march.

Let not those who are practicing meditation ever feel aghast at what they have to accomplish. When they enter the spiritual field and courageously start their honest efforts at hastening the fulfillment of their evolution, a great divine Power comes to help them at every turn. The teacher laughs at our inexplicable fears: "Even a mountain can be slowly, slowly reduced to powder; even a rocky hillock can be blasted by repeatedly shooting arrows at it: that is the glory of continuous practice. Even an ignorant one can gain wisdom."[5] This is the unfailing reward of steady, daily practice, sincerely undertaken for a long, continuous period of time.

Be regular. Be sincere. Get involved in your spiritual practice. Keep cheerful, carefree, and inspired all through your study, during your reflection, and in your devotion. Forget to worry over the future. Refuse to have regrets over the past. Surrender the present problems to His care: "Narayana, Narayana." Live in the confidence of His guiding support. Quietly, sincerely, continuously strive on, as best as you can, to live in the awareness of the infinite Self.

Let your life in the world be no more than a minor disturbance in you, the infinite Self, who is not contained in a mere body, who cannot be tantalized by the frolicsome dancings of the mind or the unpredictable, mad fancies of the intellect. Be firm, steady, undisturbed in all conditions. Nothing in this world is permanent; the disturbing factors also cannot remain permanently with you to give you perpetual disturbance. They too are finite. Then why worry? In spite of them, be regular. Be determined to pursue in unabated joy your daily meditation.

In life we all silently suffer a thousand horrid pains and impossible disturbances, and still we pursue with gusto our worldly

---

[5] From *Yoga Vāsiṣṭha*.

activities. Why not, then, suffer—with a heart filled with self-confidence and held in an attitude of dignified indifference toward all tyrannies of the flesh—the rising of passions and the storms of sentiments, and still continue our pursuit of the divine goal? Let no situation in life dare stand between us and our attempts at exploring the subtler spheres of the higher Consciousness.

Asks a rishi in utter amazement, "We suffer silently wounds inflicted by weapons, suffer the pains of diseases, yet to suffer the thought 'I am not the ego,' why such a dread? Is it so tiring and terrible, terrifying and trying?"[6]

Let not any seeker abandon his efforts in despair and run away from his meditation seat, even after his millionth failure to quiet the mind! These very attempts, though apparently unrewarding, are slowly eating away the delusions and widening the gateway to Self-realization. Never give up, never despair. Strive on! Every effort you put forth is a step taken toward the Truth. When tired, smile! When exhausted, rest! And then strive again! When dispirited, sing His glories. When totally disgusted, surrender to Him. Help comes. Help surely comes!

The path of spiritual unfoldment is reserved for the wise heroes and not for simple-minded, foolish cowards. You must, now and then, assume a get-tough stance with the mind. Don't yield. Continuously fight. Even when you are losing, retreat, but fighting for every inch. Call up reinforcements from the Lord through your devotion and surrender.

You must continue your practice until you achieve the realization of the flameless Light of Consciousness. Says the guru: "To gain the supreme experience through a total quietude of the entire mind-intellect equipment, Oh, sinless one, strive on until you reach the abode of peace, *Brahman*."[7]

Having thus set the student on the path and having equipped the pilgrim with all knowledge, the teacher in the Upanishad says to the seeker: "Godspeed. Good luck en route. May you go pleasantly beyond the kingdom of darkness"[8] into the Light of lights, by whose Light alone all other lights are ever lit up.

Never hurry. Have faith in the Lord and your teacher. And hasten slowly. "Hari Om, Hari Om, Hari Om!"

---

[6] From *Yoga Vāsiṣṭha*.
[7] From *Yoga Vāsiṣṭha*.
[8] From *Muṇḍaka Upaniṣad*.

Appendix:
My Spiritual Diary

My Spiritual Diary

See Chapter 26 for details.

	Hours of Sleep	Time of Awakening	Duration of Concentration	Books Being Read	Duration of Satsang
Day					
1					
2					
3					
4					
5					
6					
7					
8					
9					
10					
11					
12					
13					
14					
15					
16					
17					
18					
19					
20					
21					
22					
23					
24					
25					
26					
27					
28					
29					
30					
31					

Duration of Service	Malas of Japa	Upanishad Mantras Read	Mantras Written	Hours of Silence
Day				
1				
2				
3				
4				
5				
6				
7				
8				
9				
10				
11				
12				
13				
14				
15				
16				
17				
18				
19				
20				
21				
22				
23				
24				
25				
26				
27				
28				
29				
30				
31				

	Days of Fasting	Charity Given	Instances of Lying	Instances of Anger	Hours in Useless Company
Day					
1					
2					
3					
4					
5					
6					
7					
8					
9					
10					
11					
12					
13					
14					
15					
16					
17					
18					
19					
20					
21					
22					
23					
24					
25					
26					
27					
28					
29					
30					
31					

Day	Failures in Brahma-carya	Virtues Developed	Bad Qualities Being Eradicated	Failures in Controlling Bad Habits	Time of Retiring
1					
2					
3					
4					
5					
6					
7					
8					
9					
10					
11					
12					
13					
14					
15					
16					
17					
18					
19					
20					
21					
22					
23					
24					
25					
26					
27					
28					
29					
30					
31					

Guide to Sanskrit Transliteration and Pronunciation

Sanskrit is the language in which the teachings of Vedanta were first handed down orally, and later in written form. The language is thought to have originated from an early form of Aryan sometime around 2000 B.C. Later, in its perfected form, it became known as Sanskrit. The word *Sanskrit* is derived from the verb-root *kṛ* plus the prefix *sam*, meaning "to make perfect, to make complete."

The script used to write Sanskrit is Devanagari, which in the original means "divine city," being derived from two words, *deva*, "god, divine" and *nāgara*, "city."

The Sanskrit tradition is replete with spiritual literature from the earliest eras of Indian history. The Vedas, including the highly mystical literature of the Upanishads, all took form in the Sanskrit language. Even in current times, spiritual masters are known to write sacred literature in Sanskrit and at times even speak it. In *Meditation and Life*, as well as in many other books on the spiritual tradition of India, Sanskrit words are used abundantly, because in Sanskrit many terms were developed to describe spiritual concepts with utmost precision. Often, these Sanskrit terms have no precise equivalent in English, as, for instance, the words *māyā* (sometimes translated as "illusion") or *saṁsāra* (the endless cycle of births and deaths). Thus, in order to convey the most concise meaning possible, many teachers of Vedanta use the original Sanskrit terms in their teaching and writing, as Swami Chinmayananda has done in this book.

Sanskrit terms used in this book have been transliterated from the original Devanagari by using the international transliteration guidelines. These guidelines call for adding diacritical marks to English letters to guide the reader in correct pronunciation.

The following are the conventions used in *Meditation and Life:*

- Sanskrit words that appear within the text are printed in italic type, with diacritical marks.

- Commonly used Sanskrit words (such as *mantra* or *ashram*) have been incorporated into the English text and appear in roman type, without diacritical marks.

- Proper nouns derived from Sanskrit (such as *Vishnu* or *Upanishad*) have been incorporated into the English text in roman type, without diacritical marks. However, when those words appear as part of a Sanskrit phrase or title (such as *Taittirīya Upaniṣad*), the words appear in italic type, with diacritical marks.

  The table on the following page provides an approximation of how Sanskrit letters are pronounced.

Pronunciation of Sanskrit Letters

a	but	k	skate	ḍ	no equivalent			m	much
ā	mom	kh	Kate	ḍh	no equivalent			y	young
i	it	g	gate	ṇ	no equivalent			r	drama
ī	beet	gh	gawk	t	tell			l	luck
u	put	ṅ	sing	th	time			v	wile/vile[1]
ū	pool	c	chunk	d	duck			ś	shove
ṛ	rrrrig	ch	match	dh	dumb			ṣ	bushel
e	play	j	John	n	numb			s	so
ai	high	jh	jam	p	spin			h	hum
o	toe	ñ	bunch	ph	pin				
au	cow	ṭ	no equivalent	b	bun				
		ṭh	no equivalent	bh	rub				

ṁ   nasalization of preceding vowel

ḥ   aspiration of preceding vowel

[1] The sound made by the Sanskrit letter *v* is a cross between the English *v* and *w*.

Glossary

Advaita	Nondualistic (monistic) Vedanta.
Amātra-Om	The silence that follows the chant of the *Om*-mantra; it represents the fourth state of consciousness, the *turīya*.
ānanda	Bliss. Also see *sat-cit-ānanda*.
Ātman	The Self, pure Consciousness, the immanent aspect of the supreme Reality. This same Consciousness, when regarded as transcendent, is called *Brahman*.
avidyā	Ignorance. Nonapprehension of the supreme Reality. Macrocosmic *avidyā* is called *māyā*.
Bhagavad Gītā	"Song of God." A major scriptural poem in eighteen chapters, contained in the *Mahābhārata*. It is a dialogue between Lord Krishna and Arjuna, his friend and disciple, on the battlefield of the dynastic war between the Pandavas and Kauravas.
bhakta	One who follows the path of devotion. Also see *yoga*.
bhakti	Devotion. The path of devotion, one of the four main paths to liberation. Also see *yoga*.

bhakti yoga	See *yoga*.
Brahma	God in the aspect of Creator; one of the Hindu Trinity, the other two being Shiva and Vishnu.
brahmacarya	Continence in thought, word, and deed. Also the stage of the celibate student, the first of the four stages into which an individual's life is divided. The status of a religious aspirant who has taken the first monastic vows.
Brahman	Pure Consciousness, the transcendent, all-pervading supreme Reality.
Brahma Sūtras	Vedantic aphorisms by Vyasa. Also known as *Vedānta Sūtras*.
brahmavidyā	Knowledge of *Brahman*; the science of infinite Reality.
cit	See *sat-cit-ānanda*.
citta	That aspect of the subtle body which makes our thoughts apparent to us.
dhyāna	Meditation. Also see *rāja yoga*.
guṇa	Thought quality or texture. The three types of *guṇas* are: *sattva* (pure and serene), *rajas* (passionate and agitated), and *tamas* (dull and inactive).
jagat	The universe.
japa, japa yoga	The training imparted to the mind by concentrating on a single line of thought to the exclusion of all other thoughts. It generally consists of repeating one of God's names, a mantra, with the help of a *mala*, a rosary.
jīva	The individual soul; the individuality or ego in

a human being; *Ātman* identified with the body, mind, and senses.

jīvanmukta   One who has attained liberation while in the body.

jñāna   Divine Knowledge, wisdom. The path of knowledge, one of the four main paths to liberation. Also see *yoga*.

jñāna yoga   See *yoga*.

jñānī   One who follows the path of knowledge. Also, a liberated person, a knower of *Brahman*.

karma   The sum of the effects of past actions; a sequence of cause and effect on the moral plane. Action, work.

karma yoga   See *yoga*.

karma yogi   One who follows the path of action. Also see *yoga*.

loka   World, field of experience, plane of existence.

Mahābhārata   A long epic poem, attributed to Vyasa, relating to the events of a dynastic war between the Pandavas and Kauravas. It illustrates the truths of the *Vedas* and includes the great philosophic poem, the *Bhagavad Gītā*.

mahatma   "Great Soul." A monk or highly advanced master.

mālā   Prayer beads used by the Hindus, generally consisting of 108 beads strung together on a single cord with a small space between the individual beads. One of the beads, called the *meru*, is left protruding.

mantra	A chosen name of God that a seeker repeats to himself to purify his mind.
māyā	Illusion; ignorance or nonapprehension of Reality. It is described as an inexplicable power inherent in the supreme Reality, as heat is inherent in fire. Etymologically derived, the word *māyā* means "that which is not."
meru	One of the 108 beads of the Hindu *mala*, which is left protruding to mark the end of one cycle of mantra-chanting. The *meru* is never crossed; when the *meru* is reached in the telling-of-the-beads, the *mala* is turned around and the rotation, along with the chanting, is resumed.
Narayana	A name of Vishnu.
Om	Sometimes spelled *Aum*. Sacred syllable that represents the supreme Reality. Repetition of the syllable combined with meditation on its meaning is considered an effective spiritual practice.
prāṇa	Primal energy from which mental and physical energies are evolved.
Praṇava	The word-symbol of the supreme Reality—*Om*.
prema	Selfless love; ecstatic love of God.
puruṣārtha	Self-effort, a faculty unique to human beings, which helps them to choose their actions regardless of their inborn tendencies, the *vāsanās*.
rajas	One of the three thought textures (*guṇas*) that characterize the human personality. The *rājasic* quality is characterized by activity, passion, and agitation.

rāja yoga

A type of *yoga* expounded by Patanjali that focuses on concentration and meditation as a path. *Rāja yoga* has eight limbs:
1. *yama* (self-control)
2. *niyama* (observance of virtues)
3. *āsana* (postures)
4. *prāṇāyāma* (control of breath)
5. *pratyāhāra* (withdrawal of the mind)
6. *dhāraṇā* (concentration)
7. *dhyāna* (meditation)
8. *samādhi* (absorption)

rishi

Sage, seer.

sādhanā

Any spiritual practice, such as reading the scriptures, meditating, distributing one's wealth to the needy, or withdrawing one's mind from worldly pursuits.

samādhi

"Tranquil mind." A state of absorption or thoughtlessness in which a person experiences his identity with the supreme Reality.

saṁsāra

The endless cycle of births and deaths, of confusions and chaos, which human beings experience before they realize their identity with the supreme Reality.

sandhyā

The blending point of day and night, marking the times of the morning and evening worship performed by orthodox Hindus every day.

sannyāsī

A renunciate; one who has taken the vow of *sannyāsa.*

sat

Existence. Also see *sat-cit-ānanda.*

sat-cit-ānanda

Absolute existence-knowledge-bliss, an epithet for *Brahman.*

satsang	"Good company." Maintenance of contact with the higher values of life, either by association with noble persons or with inspiring writings and ideas.
sattva	One of the three thought textures (*guṇas*) that characterize the human personality. The *sāttvic* quality is characterized by purity and serenity.
Shiva	God in the aspect of Destroyer; one of the Hindu Trinity, the other two being Vishnu and Brahma.
śraddhā	Faith informed by understanding. The capacity to realize, through effort, the deeper significance of the scriptures. A sincere urgency to master the mind.
Sphota	The Logos, the sound-essence that is the controlling principle of the universe and whose symbol is *Om*.
svādhyāya	Study.
tamas	One of the three thought textures (*guṇas*) that characterize the human personality. The *tāmasic* quality is characterized by dullness and inactivity.
turīya	"The fourth." The fourth state of consciousness, which transcends the three ordinary states of consciousness—the waking, dreaming, and deep-sleep states.
upanayana	A ceremony during which a boy takes vows to observe purity, truthfulness, and self-restraint, and after which he is considered a full participant in the Hindu faith.
Upanishads (*Upaniṣads*)	The final, philosophic portion of each of the four Vedas; they constitute the quintessence of scrip-

tural truths. In all, 108 Upanishads have been preserved.

vairāgya	Dispassion; indifference to worldly things.
vāsanās	Inborn dispositions and motivating urges deep in the unconscious; the impressions formed in the personality when one acts in the world with egocentric desires.
Vedanta	"End of the Vedas." One of the six systems of Hindu philosophy, evolved from the Upanishads, the end portion of the Vedas. As the word *veda* means "knowledge," *Vedanta* can also denote "the end of knowledge" or "the most profound knowledge." Vedanta teaches that the purpose of our life is to realize the supreme Reality.
Vedas	Four ancient scriptural textbooks, compiled by the poet-sage Vyasa from prophetic declarations handed down from teacher to taught over many generations.

The four books are the *Rg Veda*, the *Yajur Veda*, the *Sāma Veda*, and the *Atharva Veda*, each of which is divided into four sections: *Mantras* (lyrical chants adoring the beauty of Nature); *Brāhmaṇas* (elaborate descriptions of rituals); *Āraṇyakas* (prescriptions for methods of subjective worship); *Upaniṣads* (philosophic declarations of the highest spiritual truths).

vidyā	Knowledge.
Vishnu	God in the aspect of Preserver; one of the Hindu Trinity, the other two being Shiva and Brahma.
viveka	Discrimination between the ephemeral objects of the world and the eternal Principle of life.

Vyāhṛtis	The three worlds or planes of existence (Bhur, Bhuvar, Svar) in which a limited ego is born, dies, and reincarnates.

yoga

The word *yoga* comes from the root *yuj*, "to join, to yoke." The joining of the self to the supreme Self. Also the techniques that promote one's progress toward the realization of the Supreme. Four of the major yogas (techniques, paths) are:

1. *Bhakti yoga*, the path of devotion, is the most fitting path for those whose heart is relatively more developed than the head. A *bhakta* is one who follows the path of devotion.

2. *Hatha yoga* deals primarily with the control of breath and the culture of the body through a system of physical exercises and postures.

3. *Jñāna yoga*, the path of knowledge, is the most fitting path for those whose head is more developed than the heart. Through discrimination, the seeker differentiates between the Real and the unreal and finally comes to realize his identity with the supreme Reality. A *jñānī* is a follower of the path of knowledge.

4. *Karma yoga*, the path of action, is most fitting for those of mixed temperament—whose head and heart are equally developed. The seeker performs selfless activity, dedicating all his actions to a higher ideal and giving up all sense of agency. A *karma yogi* is a selfless worker who follows the path of action.

About the Author

Swami Chinmayananda (1916-1993) dedicated his life to creating a renaissance of spiritual and cultural values in the country of his birth, India. He is often compared to Adi Shankaracharya, the greatest exponent of Vedanta, who thirteen centuries ago brought about a spiritual revival in India.

Born in 1916 in Kerala, India, Swami Chinmayananda was a world-renowned authority on the scriptures of India, especially the *Bhagavad Gītā* and the Upanishads. The year 1993, when he attained *Mahasamādhi* and passed from the physical plane of existence, marked forty-one years of his work as a teacher of Vedanta, a tradition of teaching that unfolds the underlying philosophic principles behind all the major religions of the world. Since the mid-sixties, his talk series, called *yajñas*, had been enjoyed worldwide, as he lectured throughout the United States, Canada, Europe, the Middle East, the Far East, Australia, and Africa.

Swami Chinmayananda began his study of Vedanta as a skeptical journalist under the tutelage of Swami Sivananda and Swami Tapovanam. His studies finished, he returned to the teeming cities of India to expound the ancient scriptural texts in English to college students, business people, and the public at large. He was the head of a worldwide organization called Chinmaya Mission, which was his vehicle for not only spreading the message of Vedanta but also for overseeing numerous cultural, educational, and social-service activities such as: the publication of books and audio and video tapes; institutes of Vedantic study; ashrams; the sponsoring of seminars, lecture series, and spiritual retreats across the globe; and the administration of schools, hospitals, orphan-ages, homes for the elderly, forest sanctuaries, and village improvement projects. Swami Tejomayananda, one of Swami Chinmayananda's senior disciples, is now continuing his guru's work as head of Chinmaya Mission worldwide.

Swami Chinmayananda started out his life as Balakrishna Menon in South India, in the state of Kerala, as the eldest son of a prominent judge. After finishing his intermediate stud-ies in science at Maharaja College in Ernakulam, he went to Trichur to study arts at St. Thomas College. Thereafter, he attended Madras University and was graduated in 1939 with degrees in science and political science. He then went to Lucknow in North India to take postgraduate degrees in literature and law. After graduation, Balakrishna Menon chose journalism rather than law as his career. He joined Nehru's newspaper, the *National Herald*, becoming a regular feature writer. While working at the *National Herald*, he actively joined India's independence movement and was imprisoned. In prison, he became seriously ill and was transferred to a hospital, where he chanced upon some articles by Swami Sivananda, which aroused both his interest and his skepticism.

After his release from prison, Balakrishna Menon went to the Himalayas to seek out Swami Sivananda, though he later said, "I went not to gain knowledge but to find out how the swamis were keeping up the bluff among the masses." In the Himalayas, the young skeptic turned enthusiast and finally renunciate monk, assuming the monastic name of Swami Chinmayananda. Soon thereafter, he sought out one of the greatest Vedantic masters of his time, Swami Tapovanam of Uttarkashi, and devoted the next several years of his life to an intensive study of the scriptures.

Swami Chinmayananda is the author of more than thirty books on Vedanta, most of them published in India. In the summer of 1991 he completed a video-taped commentary on the complete *Bhagavad Gītā*, which spans more than one hundred hours of lectures held at a Chinmaya Mission center of study and work called Krishnalaya, in Piercy, California.

Other Books by Swami Chinmayananda

Introductory Books

Art of Living
Art of Man-Making
I Love You
Kindle Life
Manual of Self-Unfoldment
Satsang with Swami Chinmayananda
Vedanta through Letters
We Must

Commentaries on Texts by Shankara

Atma Bodha
Bhaja Govindam
Forgive Me (Sivaparadhaksamapanastotram)
Hymn to Dakshinamoorthy
Sadhana Panchakam
Vakya Vritti
Vivekachoodamani

Commentaries on the Major Upanishads

Aitreya Upanishad
Isavasya Upanishad
Kaivalya Upanishad
Katha Upanishad
Kena Upanishad
Mandukya Upanishad (and Karika)
Mundaka Upanishad
Prasna Upanishad
Taittiriya Upanishad

Miscellaneous Texts

Art of Meditation
Ashtavakara Geeta
Geeta for Children
Holy Geeta
Maya and Maneesha Panchakam
Meditation, Gateway to Freedom
My Trek through Uttarkhand
Narada Bhakti Sutra
Purusha Sooktam
Vishnu Sahasranama (with commentary)

Books Translated into Other Languages

Hindi

Atma Vikaski Nirdeshak
Atma Bodha
Holy Geeta
Manav Nirmana Kala

Telegu

Atma Bodha
Bhaja Govindam
Dhyanamu-Jeevitamu
Holy Geeta
Katha Upanishad
Mandukya Upanishad (and Karika)
Mundaka Upanishad

Gujarati

Atma Bodha
Bhaja Govindam
Geeta, Vol. I
Geeta, Vol. II
Geeta, Vol. III
Geeta, Vol. IV
Jeevan Jyoti Jalao (Kindle Life)
Jeevan Vikas Marg Darsan (Self-Unfoldment)
Kshama Karo

Index